THE OFFICIAL

Harvard Student Agencies

BARTENDING COURSE

THE OFFICIAL

Harvard Student Agencies

BARTENDING COURSE

New and Revised Edition

•

Harvard Student Agencies, Inc.

Eric Witt and Geoff Rodkey, editors

Illustrated by Laura D. Schultz

St. Martin's Griffin
New York

THE OFFICIAL HARVARD STUDENT AGENCIES BARTENDING COURSE, REVISED EDITION. Copyright © 1984, 1995 by Harvard Student Agencies, Inc. All rights reserved. Printed in the United States of America. No part of this book may be used or reproduced in any manner whatsoever without written permission except in the case of brief quotations embodied in critical articles or reviews. For information, address St. Martin's Press, 175 Fifth Avenue, New York, N.Y. 10010.

Design: Judith A. Stagnitto

Library of Congress Cataloging-in-Publication Data

The official Harvard Student Agencies bartending course /
Harvard Student Agencies, Inc.—[New and rev. 2nd ed.]
      p.   cm.
    ISBN 0-312-11370-6 (pbk.)
      1. Bartending.   2. Cocktails.   I. Harvard Student
Agencies.
TX951.O34   1994
641.8'74—dc20   94-18492
                                                      CIP

Second Edition: January 1995

10   9   8   7   6   5   4   3   2

Books are available in quantity for promotional or premium use. Write to Director of Special Sales, St. Martin's Press, 175 Fifth Avenue, New York, N.Y. 10010, for information on discounts and terms, or call toll-free (800) 221-7945. In New York, call (212) 674-5151 (ext. 645).

CONTENTS

Introduction

In THE BEGINNING there was darkness, and from the darkness came a divine voice: "Let there be alcohol." And there was, and it was good—but that didn't seem to help the darkness. As soon as there was light, fire, and a whole bunch of other good things, there arose the need for a person who could master the art of drinkmaking to the same degree as a master blacksmith. These early masters of the trade (if you could actually call them masters) were a pitiful preliminary to today's Master Mixologists. Years and years would pass before innocent drinkers could be sure exactly what was in their gin and tonic.

That's where we come in. We're the folks who run the Harvard Student Agencies Bartending Course. Over the past nineteen years, we've taught over 32,000 aspiring drinkmakers how to tell the difference between a screwdriver and a gin and tonic, how to make the perfect Manhattan, how to throw a good cocktail party and, most importantly, how to get a real bartending job. And now we want to teach you, whether you're aiming to become a professional bartender, to earn a little money part-time, or just to impress your friends.

Bartending is a very simple art, and this book is designed to show you the ropes as quickly and efficiently as possible. In Chapter 1, you'll learn the basics behind any bar—what and where everything is—from mixers and utensils to garnishes and glassware. In Chapter 2, we'll show you how to mix basic drinks. In Chapter 3, we list all the drink recipes you'll ever need. In Chapter 4, we'll show you how to throw a cocktail party for any occasion and any group, large or small. In Chapter 5, you'll find a brief but comprehensive history of alcohol. In Chapter 6, we discuss the more serious side of drinking, from hangovers and alcoholism to drunk driving and the bartender's legal responsibilities. Finally, in Chapter 7, we'll show you what it takes to get a job as a professional bartender.

CHAPTER 1

The Basics

If YOU'VE NEVER set foot behind a fully stocked bar before, your first encounter with one might be somewhat bewildering. Row upon row of mysterious bottles, a dozen different types of glassware, various utensils, some garnishes, a few seasonings, and a bizarre appliance that looks like the result of an unholy union between a Slinky and a spatula.

Relax. None of this is as complicated as it seems. Most bartenders never even use most of the bottles that you'll find in a fully stocked bar. A few simple guidelines will allow you to master the different glasses in no time at all. And that funny-looking thing? It's a cocktail strainer. Perfectly harmless.

In this chapter, we'll explain the various elements that make up any bar, starting with the basic bar setup—the simple layout that's similar for bars of all shapes and sizes—and then moving on to brief descriptions of the various utensils, glassware, and garnishes that you'll need to tend bar. At the end of the chapter, you'll find a brief collection of common bartending terms.

Basic Bar Setup

If you've ever looked closely at a professional bar or someone's well-stocked home bar, you've probably noticed that bottles are generally kept in two main areas: the "front bar" and the "back bar." A good bottle arrangement enables bartenders to make drinks efficiently, without having to search all over the place for the bottle they need next.

At the front bar, also known as the "cocktail party bar" or the "speed bar," bartenders mix more than 70 percent of their drinks. As these names suggest, all the basic, most popular drinks can be made using the bottles located in this area.

A typical front bar setup is shown on page 5: Rum, vodka, tequila, and gin—the light alcohols—go on the right. If you're serving drinks to a young crowd, you'll find that light alcohols are more popular than dark and should be placed according to your handedness: on the right for right-handed people and on the left for southpaws. This arrangement allows for slightly greater speed, which is a crucial component in bartending. On the left are bourbon, blended whiskey, and Scotch—the dark alcohols. In the middle, dry vermouth and sweet vermouth. The dry vermouth stands next to the gin so that you can quickly make a martini with the two, and the sweet vermouth is next to the blended whiskey so you can just as rapidly mix a Manhattan. The row of empty circles represents the "show row," which is found on some professional and large home bars. It is exactly the same as those behind it, except that each remains sealed and has the label facing the guests so they can read what brands the bartender pours. The show row really doesn't have an official function other than to inform guests what is being served, and it is often omitted.

This setup, while common, is not absolute. Depending on the alcohol preferences of your guests, it is generally safe to say that the best setup involves placing the bottles that will

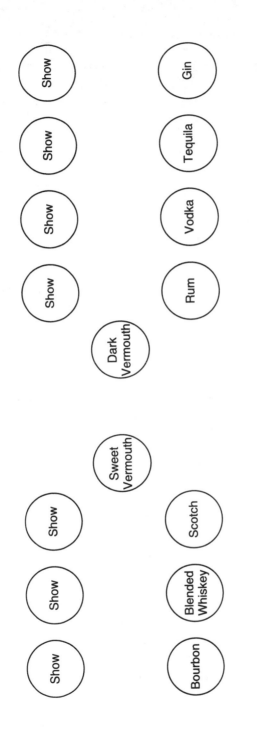

FRONT BAR SETUP

be used the most within easy reach. For example, in the diagram on page 7, the bartender alternated light and dark alcohols and kept the vermouths to the side. This setup is most useful at parties where a lot of drinks with dark alcohols are served as well as martinis and Manhattans.

You can often design your own organization of the front of the bar, especially when working alone. The key to any setup is efficiency—place the bottles so you can find them as quickly as possible. Also, you might want to keep the most frequently used bottles on the side that corresponds to your handedness. (For more detailed diagrams, including garnish and mixer placements, see pages 138–41.)

In professional bars, a "speed rack" usually replaces the front bar. This rack, attached to the bar or sink directly in front of the bartender, holds "house brands" (usually less expensive brands) of front-bar liquor. The bartender uses house liquor for every drink unless the customer specifies a well-known brand, or "call brand" as it's known in bartending lingo. The more expensive call brands stay on the back bar.

The back bar, also called the "liqueur bar," contains liqueurs, brandies, and other less frequently ordered liquors. As the name suggests, bartenders usually keep those bottles behind them, since they rarely have to use these liquors and don't mind walking a few extra steps when they need them.

At first glance, the back bar appears to be a confusing array of bottles, apparently thrown onto the shelves in random order. Actually, the organization of the back bar follows two basic and sensible rules:

Rule 1: Keep bottles on the back bar separated by flavor base. For example, put the four orange-flavored liqueurs together, the Kahlúa next to the coffee-flavored brandy, and all the call brands of Scotch near each other. Chapter 5 contains descriptions of each liquor and lists of liqueurs by flavor base.

Rule 2: Keep bottles used for the same drink together whenever possible. For example, keep the brandy next to the crème de menthe so you can quickly grab both of them to

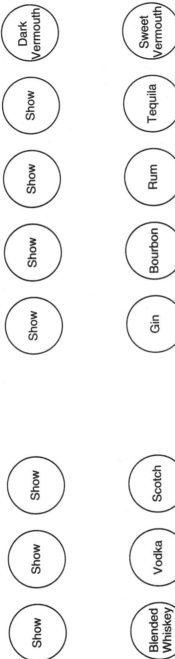

Dark Vermouth · Show · Show · Show · Show

Sweet Vermouth · Tequila · Rum · Bourbon · Gin

Show · Show

Scotch · Vodka · Blended Whiskey

BARTENDER

ALTERNATE FRONT BAR SETUP

make a stinger. Chapter 3 will give you an idea of the more common liquor combinations.

Utensils

Bartenders usually keep a variety of tools around to help them do everything from shaking to straining to pouring. The most basic and useful utensils comprise what we like to call the "bartending kit"; most bartenders would never try to work without them. (To order your own official Harvard Bartending Kit, see page 215.)

A basic kit contains:

Shaker set: Bartenders use a shaker to make whiskey sours, daiquiris, margaritas, and the other popular shaken drinks listed in Chapter 3. We prefer a steel shell for the outer part and a glass shaker that fits inside. Glass works best for the inner part because some recipes ask you to "eyeball" the right amount of liquor in a drink, and glass allows you to see how much you pour. Shakers come in many shapes and sizes; here at Harvard Student Agencies, we prefer a 12-ounce shaker because it allows the bartender to prepare several servings of a drink at once. However, use what is comfortable for you and allows you to make drinks with the greatest speed and efficiency.

Strainer: The strainer fits over the shaker so you can pour the chilled drink into a glass without the ice cubes. This type of drink is referred to as "straight up," as in a martini straight up.

Shaker

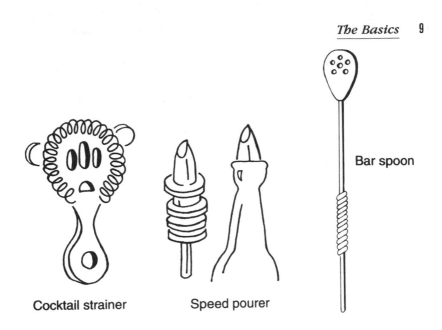

Cocktail strainer   Speed pourer   Bar spoon

Speedpourers: Speedpourers fit into the mouth of a bottle and dispense the liquor at an even rate. As you will see in Chapter 2, these gadgets are essential for the speed-oriented bartender. Make sure to put the speedpourer in the bottle at a right angle to the label; with all the pourers facing the same way, you can quickly grab each bottle without having to check the direction of the stream of liquor. By positioning the bottles this way, customers are able to read the label as you pour, and it also ensures that liquor flows out at an even rate.

Bar spoon: The bar spoon we recommend looks like the one shown here—with a long, twirled handle and a small spoon at the end. This type of spoon serves three purposes: you can stir drinks with the handle, pour alcohol carefully down the twirled segment (when making pousse-cafés, for example), and pick up fruit with the spoon. Although busy bartenders rarely follow the rule, the law in some states prohibits the handling of fruit garnishes, so the spoon is made for those law-abiding bartenders.

Combination Corkscrew/Bottle opener/Can opener: We like to use this tool because three separate pieces can get lost too easily at a hectic bar. You should choose whatever feels most comfortable.

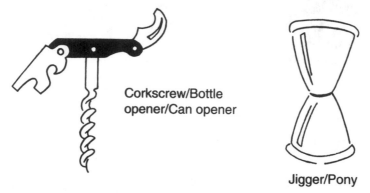

Corkscrew/Bottle opener/Can opener

Jigger/Pony

Jigger/Pony: The larger end is the jigger, which measures 1½ ounces; the smaller end is the pony, which measures 1 ounce. Although sometimes quite handy, a jigger/pony or other measuring glass is unnecessary when you have speed-pourers. Some bars, however, insist that employees use measuring glasses to ensure that they don't pour too much and waste liquor.

The following items are also useful:

Ice bucket: Bucket, basin, bag or whatever you have around for holding ice—anything clean is fine.

Ice scoop or tongs: They are nice for some occasions, though impractical in a busy bar.

Knife: You will need a knife to cut up fruit garnishes.

Glassware

The following list and illustrations will familiarize you with some glassware options available in bars. For the home, purchase any or all of them. In a professional establishment, the manager usually decides which glass to use for each drink. These illustrations are merely examples of different types; you'll find many variations and creative adaptations from bar to bar. Be careful, though—don't be too creative. Remember, the right glass makes quite a difference in the final appearance of a drink—wine loses some of its appeal in a beer mug, and a piña colada won't fit in a shot glass.

Highball: Used for more drinks than any other glass (for all those gin and tonics, Scotch and waters, etc.), highballs vary considerably from bar to bar. Most are clear, tall glasses that hold between 8 and 12 ounces.

Lowball

Highball

Lowball: Also used for many drinks, lowball or "on-the-rocks" glasses come in different shapes and designs. Most hold 4 to 9 ounces and are best for drinks served on the rocks—martini on the rocks, Scotch on the rocks, Black Russian, and many others.

Old Fashioned: This 4- to 7-ounce glass looks similar to an on-the-rocks glass, but has a bump in the base to remind the bartender to prepare the sugar, water, and bitters mixture for an Old Fashioned. Today, many bars use these to do double duty as on-the-rocks glasses.

Collins: Best for Collinses, sloe gin fizzes, and Singapore slings, these 12-ounce glasses are frosted with some clear glass left at the top to remind the bartender to add soda water to the top of a Collins. They lend a cool, refreshing image to these drinks.

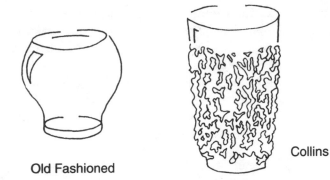

Old Fashioned

Collins

Cocktail/Whiskey sour: Martinis, Manhattans, and other cocktails ordered straight up are initially prepared with ice and then strained into a 4-ounce cocktail glass. Sours are prepared in the same way and strained into a 4-ounce sour glass. The stem on these glasses enables the drinker to hold the glass without warming the chilled contents.

Cocktail   Whiskey Sour

Wine: Wineglasses come in a wide array of shapes and sizes. Choose yours according to your own preferences.

Sherry: Serve sherry, port, or apéritifs like Dubonnet in 2½- to 3½-ounce glasses.

Wine

Sherry

Champagne: Champagne glasses come in two shapes and sizes. The American glass, by far the most popular here, is very wide and shallow and holds 4 to 6 ounces. The European glass, tall and fluted, has a 7- to 11-ounce capacity. The European glass is better for champagne than its American counterpart because the tapered mouth has less surface area and thus holds the bubbles in longer (unlike the American glass, which allows the bubbles to dissipate quickly). Also, the European glass causes less spillage.

American/European
Champagne

Beer: Usually holding about 10 ounces, beer glasses come in two basic shapes, the mug and the Pilsner glass. Most people have already seen mugs. The Pilsner-style glass was invented for use with Pilsner beer (see page 167), but it is actually suitable for any kind. Bar managers often prefer mugs because they do not break as easily as the Pilsners.

Beer Mug/Pilsner   Liqueur

Liqueur: Also known as a "pony," this 1-ounce glass is appropriate for after-dinner liqueurs and pousse-cafés.

Shot: These 1- to 2-ounce glasses can be used to serve shots of liquor or to measure alcohol.

Brandy: Brandy snifters range in capacity from 5 to 25 ounces. All have basically the same shape, and are designed to be cupped by the hand to warm the brandy.

Shot   Brandy

Miscellaneous: You know the type—coconut shells in Polynesian restaurants, free tumblers from the gas station, glasses with big mouse ears from that vacation in Orlando . . .

Garnishes, Garbage, Mixers, and Other Additions

Just as the right glassware can make a cocktail look infinitely more appealing, those additions the bartender puts in a drink also make it look—and taste—better.

The words "garnish" and "garbage" refer to the fruits and vegetables you put in a drink. Although many bartenders use the two words interchangeably, technically they have different meanings. Garnishes change the taste of a drink, such as a lime wedge in a gin and tonic or a lemon twist in a bourbon. Garbage just makes the drink look pretty, such as a cherry in a Manhattan or an orange slice and pineapple chunk in a piña colada. Here are some garnishes and garbage commonly found on a bar:

Lemon twists: Cut off the two ends of the lemon. With a spoon, force the fruit out one end. (You just use the peel in the drink.) Slice the peel lengthwise into quarter-inch wide strips. Twist the peel over the drink, rub it around the edge of the glass, drop it in, and stir. It's a good idea to keep some lemon slices or wedges at the bar, in case some fussy drinkers drop by who prefer a more lemony taste.

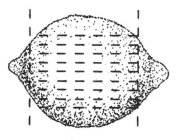

Lemon

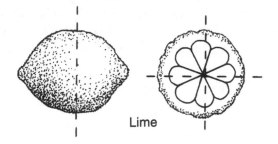

Lime

Lime wedges: Cut the lime in half (through its equator) and then quarter each half, following the natural contours of the fruit, to make eight wedges. Squeeze the lime over the drink, rub it around the edge of the glass if you like, and drop it in. Lime wedges are popular garnishes in many drinks, so keep plenty on hand. If you start to run low on limes, cut smaller wedges, but make sure you don't run out.

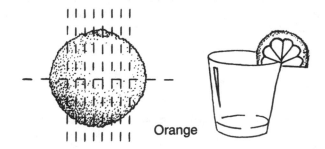

Orange

Orange slices: Starting at the stem, cut the orange in half. Lay each half with the flat side down, and cut widthwise to make semicircular, fanlike slices. Make a little cut down the middle of each slice so that you can slide it onto the rim of the glass.

Cherries: Use stemmed maraschino cherries in your cocktails. Drinkers like stems so they can easily pull the cherry out of their glass.

Olives: A must for the martini drinker, olives should be green, pitted, and without pimento.

Onions: Get little cocktail onions for your Gibsons—unless you don't know anyone who drinks Gibsons. Many people don't.

Olives

Onion

Bartenders usually keep at least four carbonated mixers on the front bar. (The diagrams in Chapter 4 show efficient locations for these mixers.) Cola and tonic water go best with light alcohols (as in rum and Coke or gin and tonic). Soda and ginger ale mix well with dark alcohols (as in Scotch and soda or bourbon and ginger). You might also want to have other carbonated mixers at the bar, such as 7-Up or Sprite, bitter lemon, Collins mixer (although you'll learn how to make Collinses from scratch in Chapter 3), or any other of the many mixers available. Don't forget diet sodas; many people drink rum and diet cola, for example, to cut down on the extra calories.

Some people confuse soda water and tonic water, and use the two interchangeably. Avoid this mistake. Tonic contains sugar and bitter-tasting quinine. Soda water has bubbles in it and sometimes a little salt, but nothing else. Some bars also serve naturally carbonated ("sparkling") spring waters, like Perrier. Soda water, club soda, and seltzer can be used interchangeably for the most part. Recently, more and more flavored varieties of soda water have been introduced. While these drinks may be used occasionally as a substitute for soda water and a garnish (such as a lime), they are not usually used behind a bar.

Bottled mixers will suffice for the home bar or for a small, relaxed corner pub; soda taps work well in medium-size, moderately busy bars; but when dealing with large, crowded, high-pressure establishments, only a "soda gun" keeps the mixer flowing fast enough. Also known as an "arm" or a "snake," this dispenser consists of a long, flexible tube with a set of buttons on the end. Each button represents a mixer; the bartender merely pushes a button, and the desired soda gushes out of the gun. This device eliminates the inefficient hassle of searching all over the place for bottles, uncapping them, and running out every two minutes. If you work in a bar with a snake, ask the manager or a co-worker to show you how to set it up and make minor repairs.

Juices, of course, also go well with many liquors. Some popular mixing juices are orange, grapefruit, pineapple, cranberry, and tomato.

Many drinks, such as Collinses, sours, and daiquiris, call for "sour" or "bar" mix. This mixer contains lemon juice, sugar, and some egg white to make the drink slightly foamy (see page 27 for the recipe). Sour mix often comes in powdered form (Quik-Lem, for example); in a pinch you can substitute frozen lemonade mixed with half the prescribed water.

Other mixers include:

Rose's lime juice: A reconstituted lime juice used most often in gimlets. Rose's is sweetened, so do not substitute it in recipes calling for plain lime juice.

Cream: Don't use anything heavier than light cream or half-and-half, or you'll fill the drinker's stomach too quickly.

Milk: For Sombreros, especially. It can be used as a substitute for cream.

Water: To mix with whiskey. If your bar does not dispense water through a tap or a snake, keep water in a pitcher so all the air will dissipate. Otherwise, drinks will appear cloudy from the tiny air bubbles in tap water.

You'll find a wide variety of condiments and other additions on a well-stocked bar. These include:

Sugar: Buy superfine granulated sugar, which mixes more easily in drinks and won't leave a syrupy layer on the bottom of the glass.

Simple syrup: An alternative to dry sugar. Some bartenders prefer to make simple syrup by mixing sugar and water together. Heat 1 pound of sugar in 1 quart of water until it dissolves. Keep it in a bottle with a speedpourer in it.

Salt: Keep a plate of rock, not table, salt on hand for making Salty Dogs and margaritas.

Grenadine: This red, nonalcoholic sugar-and-pomegranate syrup colors and sweetens drinks.

Bitters: As the name suggests, this mixer is bitter and infrequently used in drinks these days except in Old Fashioneds. You can add it to Manhattans or Bloody Marys if you like. Please note that bitters is alcoholic and should not be used in nonalcoholic drinks as even a few drops can be harmful to some nondrinkers.

Bloody Mary mixings: Keep any or all of the following on hand for Bloodies: Tabasco sauce, Worcestershire sauce, salt and pepper, horseradish, celery stalks.

Nutmeg: For brandy Alexanders and eggnogs.

And, of course, the most important addition: *ice* (lots of it).

This rather extensive list of garnishes, mixers, and condiments should give you an idea of the kinds of ingredients to expect in Chapter 3. Don't run out to the store and buy every one of them, though; just pick and choose according to your preferences.

Terminology

Bartenders (and drinkers) love to throw around jargon to make their jobs or lives sound more interesting than they really are, but some of the following words are indispensable for communicating exactly what you want to order or mix.

Dash/Splash: This refers to the amount of something in a drink, such as a dash of Tabasco sauce or a splash of water. Technically, a dash equals ⅙ teaspoon (a few drops) and a splash equals ½ ounce (a long squirt), but a bartender very rarely measures these small amounts.

Shot: A shot is no precise amount; it usually ranges from 1 to 2 ounces depending on the bar and the size of its shot glasses. A shot is also a type of drink.

Jigger: Measures 1½ ounces.

Pony: Measures 1 ounce. A pony is also a type of glass.

Nip: Nips are little bottles of liquor, popular as gifts at holiday time and as drink servings on airplanes (where they are also called miniatures). They come in three sizes: 1-ounce, 1.6-ounce, and 2-ounce.

Fifth: The traditional size of the American liquor bottle, now largely superseded by the 750-milliliter bottle; ⅕ gallon = ⅘ quart = 25.6 ounces.

Proof: Proof is twice the percentage of alcohol. For example, 100 proof equals 50 percent alcohol. This term indicates the strength of the liquor. The proof of a drink may range from 0 to 200 with an average mixed drink being about 80 proof, the average wine around 15 proof, and the average beer running about 8 proof. These numbers are only rough guidelines; the actual proof of a liquor is usually listed on the label. A responsible bartender should always make sure the drinker knows what proof he or she is getting.

Grain neutral spirits (GNS): This 190-proof (95 percent pure) alcohol has no distinctive color, odor, or taste. Both vodka and gin are initially prepared as GNS and then later filtered or flavored, and cut with distilled water. In some states it is possible to buy grain in liquor stores; but be careful, one grain drink is as intoxicating as three to four ordinary drinks, yet no flavor, color, or odor signals this potency to the drinkers. GNS is very irritating to the throat and should never be drunk straight. Everclear is the most common brand name for GNS.

Neat: Alcohol served right from the bottle with no ice.

Straight up: A drink mixed in a glass with ice and then strained into another glass without ice (sometimes referred to as a chilled drink).

On the rocks: Refers to a drink with ice. In some cases, the drink is prepared as a straight-up drink, but is then strained into a rocks glass *with* ice.

Side/Back/Chaser: Some bars, instead of regular highballs, serve a glass of mixer with 1½ ounces of liquor on the side in a shot glass. This glass of mixer is called a side, back, or chaser.

Mist/Frappé: Both terms refer to a drink served over shaved ice, but a mist is generally served in a rocks glass and a frappé in a cocktail or champagne glass. For example, a "crème de menthe mist" describes crème de menthe poured over shaved ice in a rocks glass.

Dry/Sweet: Refers to the proportion of vermouth in a martini and to the kind of vermouth in a Manhattan. (See pages 51–52.)

Straight/Blended: These terms refer to whiskey. (See pages 155–56.)

Labeling: The letters on a brandy or whiskey bottle describe the contents. They are usually listed in combination. For example, VSOP on a brandy label stands for Very Special Old Pale. These letters are primarily used descriptively, but they should give you some idea of the quality of the liquor.

E— especially
F— fine
M—mellow
V— very
X— extra
C— cognac or Canadian
Q— quart
S— special (or "superior")
P— pale
O— old

Keg: (Technically, a half keg). A stainless steel beer barrel holding 15½ gallons.

Virgin: A drink prepared without liquor—for example, a Virgin Mary (Bloody Mary without vodka). For a selection of nonalcoholic drinks, see page 109–15.

Measurements: Most distillers and winemakers now use metric measurements. This list illustrates the relationship between standard and metric amounts.

Standard	*Metric*
1 pint = 16 ounces	500 milliliters = 16.9 ounces
1 fifth = 25.6 ounces	750 milliliters = 25.4 ounces
1 quart = 32 ounces	1 liter = 33.8 ounces

Other standard bottles are the magnum (52 ounces), the jeroboam (104 ounces), the rehoboam (156 ounces) and the jeromagnum (208 ounces). The last three terms are seldom used, and you may never see or hear them again. But we thought it'd be nice to close the chapter in a comprehensive manner.

CHAPTER 2

Mixing Drinks

This MAY COME as a surprise to you, but there are actually only three basic types of drinks. Of course, this doesn't include a few fairly exotic exceptions, which we'll discuss in Chapter 3. Most drinks, however, spring from variations on three simple types: highballs, stirred cocktails (or lowballs), and shaken cocktails. In this chapter, you'll proceed step by step through these three mixing techniques. As we said, you may be surprised when you realize how simple bartending really is.

Highballs

Gin and tonic, Scotch and soda, rum and Coke, screwdriver . . . sound familiar? These drinks are highballs, which comprise at least 70 percent of all drinks a typical bartender serves. When you finish reading this short section on how to make a highball, you'll be able to put together almost three-fourths of the drinks we list in Chapter 3. Some highballs require a little extra effort, but most are incredibly simple once you know the basic technique.

A highball usually measures about 9 ounces, including ice, liquor, and mixer. Serve it in—you guessed it—a highball glass. Follow these steps:

1. Fill a highball glass two-thirds full with ice.
2. Pour in one jigger (1½ ounces) of liquor. (Some bars prefer to save money by serving only 1-ounce highballs.)
3. Pour mixer to the top. If you pour too little, it looks like you're skimping. If you *are* skimping, find a way to do it discreetly.
4. If the mixer is noncarbonated, stir it, or stick a straw in and let the drinker stir it. With carbonated mixers, do not stir; the bubbles do the mixing, and stirring tends to make the carbonation go flat.
5. Garnish the drink, if necessary.

You can measure the liquor in the following three ways; the Harvard Bartending Course uses method 3.

Method 1: Measure the liquor in a jigger glass and then pour it into the drink. This method is accurate, but too slow and cumbersome if you're working at a crowded bar.

Some bar managers insist that their employees use this method to ensure that no liquor is wasted. If you must follow this procedure, here's a way to pour faster and make customers think they're getting a stronger drink. First, hold the jigger glass in one hand and the liquor bottle in the other. Pour less than 1½ ounces into the jigger glass, and then dump that into the highball glass while also pouring a little more liquor from the bottle. To the customers, it appears as though you gave them a full jigger plus another splash from the bottle in each drink. They will be pleased and probably tip you more.

Method 2: Bartenders call this the "two-finger" technique. Put your two fingers together around the bottom of the highball glass and then pour in liquor until it reaches the top of your fingers. This method is faster than the jigger glass routine, but inaccurate; bartenders with bony fingers serve weak drinks while fat-fingered types will quickly become a drinker's best friend!

Method 3: Fast, accurate . . . it's the "three-count" technique. Do you remember reading about speedpourers and how they fit into the mouth of a bottle to make the liquor come out at an even rate? With a speedpourer in, if you grab the liquor bottle by the neck, turn it completely upside down over the glass, and count to three at the right speed, you can measure out exactly 1½ ounces. Get a bottle of colored water, put a speedpourer in it, and keep practicing until you get a cadence that measures exactly 1½ ounces, or half an ounce per count.

Remember that you must grab the bottle firmly by the neck to get the best leverage and control. You must also make sure to turn the bottle completely upside down so the right amount of alcohol comes out. Practice a few times until you get it right. After a while, you won't even have to count anymore, but will pour the right amount automatically; a three-count will eventually *feel* right to you.

Also, once you develop an accurate cadence, you can use it to pour 1 ounce (a two-count), 2 ounces (a four-count), and so on. In past editions, we advocated the use of a four-count, but an even three-count for the standard shot (1½ ounces) makes one count exactly equal to half an ounce, a ratio that will come in handy with some more complex drinks with unusual measurements.

To review, here's how to make a gin and tonic:

1. Fill a highball glass two-thirds full with ice.
2. Grab the gin bottle by the neck, turn upside down and count to three.
3. Add tonic water. Fill the glass almost to the top to make it look full, but not overflowing. Don't stir—no need to stir carbonated mixers.
4. Squeeze a lime wedge over the top of the drink and drop it in.

Pretty simple, huh? You're now fully qualified to mix 70 percent of the drinks known to the world.

Stirred Cocktails

The stirred cocktail category includes drinks such as martinis, Manhattans, and gimlets. They are stronger than highballs and measure about 3 ounces of liquid.

You can make stirred cocktails two ways: straight up (or just "up") or on the rocks (or just "rocks"). Straight-up cocktails are made in a shaker glass with ice and then strained into a cocktail glass without ice. On-the-rocks drinks can be made either right in a rocks glass with ice, or stirred in a shaker and then strained into a glass with fresh ice. Practice here by making a martini up, and a gimlet on the rocks.

The martini recipe calls for about eight parts gin to one part dry vermouth.

1.   Fill the shaker glass two-thirds full with ice.
2.   Start with the ingredient you'll be using less of—in this case, dry vermouth. Remember that a stirred cocktail should contain about 3 ounces of liquid, so one-ninth of that is only a little splash of vermouth.
3.   Gin makes up the balance of the drink. Put in about a generous five-count (melting ice after stirring brings the liquid content up to 3 ounces).
4.   Stir well—very well. Remember, this drink has to stay cold and this is the only time it will have ice in it. Stir with the straight end of your bar spoon so you won't spill ice cubes all over the place.
5.   Strain the drink into a cocktail glass (or whatever glass you've chosen to serve it in). To do this, just put your strainer over the shaker glass and pour.

6. Garnish the martini with two olives (pitted and without pimentos).

You'll read more in Chapter 3 about martini variations—"dry" martinis, for example. Now make a vodka gimlet on the rocks, which contains five parts vodka to one part Rose's lime juice.

1. Fill the shaker glass two-thirds full with ice.
2. Put in a one-count of Rose's lime juice.
3. Pour in five times as much vodka as this. A typical five-count should be fine.
4. Stir well.
5. Strain the drink into an on-the-rocks glass full of fresh ice.
6. If you wish, drop in a lime wedge as a garnish.

Shaken Cocktails

This part of bartending is fun and very professional looking once you get the hang of it. When you're starting out, be wary of going overboard and spilling all over yourself and innocent bystanders.

Let's try making a whiskey sour. The recipe calls for 2 ounces of blended whiskey, the juice of half a lemon, and 1 teaspoon of sugar. But if you use a premixed bar mix or sour mix (see page 18), you will already have the lemon and sugar mixture made and bottled on your bar. Follow these steps:

1. Fill the shaker glass two-thirds full with ice.
2. Pour in 2 ounces blended whiskey—a four-count.
3. Now pour in about 1½ ounces of sour mix (depending on the sweetness of the mix and your preferences)—about a three-count.

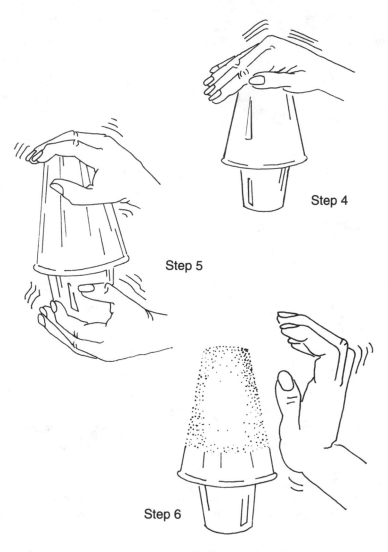

Step 4

Step 5

Step 6

4. Put the stainless steel shell over the shaker glass (as shown) and press down on the top to make a seal between the two. The steel shell is going to contract when the ice makes it cold, so the seal will get even stronger.

5. Hold the top and bottom of the shaker and shake it up and down. Eventually you can get fancy in your shaking, but always make sure the ingredients go up and down in the glass.

6. You now need to break the seal. Look for the frost line on the shell, which indicates where the seal is, and then tap the shell with the heel of your hand at the frost line. The seal makes a loud snap as it breaks, and the steel shell comes loose.

7. Keeping the shaker glass and shell together, turn the whole thing over. Then take the glass out of the steel shell. By turning the shaker over so that the shell is on the bottom you avoid making a mess.

8. Strain the drink from the shell into a whiskey sour glass or some other type of lowball glass (preferably one with a stem so the drink will stay colder longer). The strainer should fit comfortably over the mouth of the shaker to prevent ice from entering the cocktail glass.

Step 7

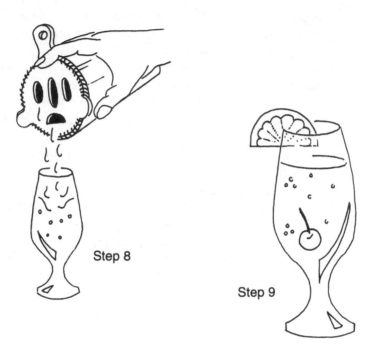

Step 8

Step 9

9.   Garnish with a cherry and an orange slice.
10. Clean the shaker: pour in some water, shake it around, dump it out, and then wipe the inside. Some shaken cocktails have milk or cream in them, in which case take special pains in cleaning the shaker—nobody likes a whiskey sour with chunks of curdled milk adrift in it.

If you plan to work professionally some day, you'll need to learn how to make several drinks at a time. This is fairly easy to do, but don't bother learning how unless you plan on speed-bartending some day. If you want to make three gin and tonics, for example, follow these directions:

1. Line up three ice-filled glasses in a row with their rims touching.
2. Turn the gin bottle over the first glass for a three-count, and then just move the bottle quickly over to the second glass and then the third.
3. Pour tonic in the three glasses.
4. Squeeze limes into the drinks.

The next time you go to a bar, watch the bartender and you'll learn other professional hints. Don't worry too much about being exact: you can't substitute whiskey for water or vodka for vermouth, but the world will not end tomorrow if you pour 2 ounces instead of 1½. As evidence of this, notice how often recipes for the same drink differ from one bar book to another, and from one bar to the next.

CHAPTER 3

Recipes

Most BARTENDING GUIDES fall all over themselves trying to convince you that their book contains more drink recipes than the competition's. "Contains All the Drink Recipes Ever Invented!" . . . "Over 400,000 Recipes!" they proudly exclaim.

Let's be reasonable. As a practicing bartender, you're probably never going to encounter 399,950 of these drinks, most of which are about as popular as vodka and mayonnaise. In this chapter, you'll find the favorites, the drinks people ask for regularly, and the classics, lesser-known recipes that every good bartender knows. We've also included a few of the newer and more trendy concoctions, some fun novelties that you may not be able to find anywhere else, and a section of tasty nonalcoholic drinks.

How to Use the Recipe Guide

Most of these recipes are categorized according to how they're made. This setup enables you to learn and remember the method at the same time that you see the actual recipe. If you want to make a specific drink, you can find it in the index.

Below we have listed thirteen main categories of drinks. The first three sections contain three subgroups: Basics, Populars, and Funs. *Basic* drinks are the old standbys, such as gin and tonic in the highball section, martinis in the stirred section, and daiquiris in the shaken section. *Popular* drinks aren't quite as classic but do require memorization if you plan to work in a bar someday. *Fun* drinks include many you've never heard of before and may never need again, so you don't need to memorize them. Fun drinks are arranged alphabetically.

The thirteen categories are:

1. Highballs
    Basic (memorize)
    Popular (memorize if you plan to work in a bar)
    Fun drinks (no need to memorize—arranged alphabetically)
2. Stirred Cocktails
    Basic
    Popular
    Fun drinks
3. Shaken Cocktails
    Basic
    Popular
    Fun drinks
4. The Latest and Greatest Drinks
5. Blended Drinks
6. Hot Drinks
7. Flaming Drinks
8. Pousse-Cafés
9. Wine and Champagne Drinks
10. Coolers
11. Beer Drinks
12. Light and Nonalcholic Drinks
13. Punch Recipes

Highballs

Serve the following drinks in a 9-ounce highball glass, unless you prefer another more creative presentation. In case you've already forgotten how to make highballs, review page 23–26.

Basic Highballs

These recipes are the most common ones you will serve, whether in a bar or at home. Memorize them. It's easy—they are arranged by liquor, in order to help you remember the ingredients.

GIN

Gin and Tonic
    1½ oz. gin
    tonic to fill
Garnish with a lime wedge.

Gin Chiller
    1½ oz. gin
    ginger ale to fill
Garnish with a lime wedge. Drinks with the word "chiller" in their name contain ginger ale as a main ingredient.

Gin Rickey
    1½ oz. gin
    soda water to fill
Garnish with a lemon twist. This is the only gin and clear mixer drink garnished with a lemon twist—most call for a lime wedge.

Orange Blossom
    1½ oz. gin
    orange juice to fill
This drink is a screwdriver with gin instead of vodka.

Tom Collins
    1½ oz. gin
    Collins mix to fill
Garnish with a cherry and an orange slice. (You'll find a more elaborate recipe for Collinses in the Shaken Cocktails section, on page 62.)

Gin and Grapefruit Juice
    1½ oz. gin
    grapefruit juice to fill

Gin Fizz
    1½ oz. gin
    7-Up or Sprite to fill
Garnish with a lime wedge.

VODKA

Vodka and Tonic
  1½ oz. vodka
  tonic water to fill
Garnish with a lime wedge.

Vodka Chiller
  1½ oz. vodka
  ginger ale to fill
Garnish with a lime wedge.

Screwdriver
  1½ oz. vodka
  orange juice to fill

Cape Codder
  1½ oz. vodka
  cranberry juice to fill
Garnish with a lime wedge.

Here's an example of how to memorize drink recipes. If you can't remember that cranberries grow on Cape Cod, Massachusetts, try to remember all those Cs: Cape Codder and cranberry juice. Learn to associate and play word games like this one so you'll have an easier time recalling ingredients and proportions when you're tending bar.

Madras

    1½ oz. vodka
    orange juice to ¾ fill
    cranberry juice to fill

Dribble cranberry juice around the top to give a mottled appearance. Don't stir. This drink should remind you of a bright madras plaid.

Sea Breeze

    1½ oz. vodka
    grapefruit juice to ¾ fill
    cranberry juice to fill

Stir. This drink is a pretty pink color.

Salty Dog

    1½ oz. vodka
    grapefruit juice to fill

Pour this drink into a highball glass rimmed with salt.

To rim a glass with salt:

1. Pour rock salt on a plate.
2. Rub a lime wedge around rim of glass.
3. Roll rim of glass around in salt.

Greybound

A salty dog without the salt.

Vodka Collins

1½ oz. vodka

Collins mix to fill

Garnish with a cherry and an orange slice. (You'll find a more elaborate recipe for Collinses in the Shaken Cocktails section, on page 62.)

Vodka and 7-Up, Sprite, or Fruit Soda

1½ oz. vodka.

7-Up, Sprite, or any fruit soda to fill

Garnish with a cherry and an orange slice.

Bloody Mary

1½ oz. vodka

tomato juice to ¾ fill

small splash lemon juice

dash Worcestershire sauce

dash Tabasco sauce (more for a hotter drink)

shake of salt and pepper

¼ tsp. horseradish (optional)

Garnish with a celery stick.

"Bloody" drinkers have diverse tastes, so you should ask if the drinker would like the drink hot, and then alter accordingly with Tabasco sauce. There are about as many different recipes for Bloody Marys as there are drinkers. Some prefer gin to vodka and any number of interesting ingredients may be added or substituted to make that perfect, customized Bloody Mary. You can experiment with clam juice, dill, basil, garlic, curry powder, or barbecue sauce. Feel free to be creative; you may be the bartender who discovers the perfect combination!

R U M

Rum and Tonic
    1½ oz. rum
    tonic water to fill
Garnish with a lime wedge.

Rum and Cola
    1½ oz. rum
    cola (or diet cola) to fill

Cuba Libre
    1½ oz. rum
    cola to fill
Garnish with a lime wedge. Cuba Libre ("free Cuba") is just a fancy name for a rum and cola with a lime wedge.

Rum Chiller
    1½ oz. rum
    ginger ale to fill
Garnish with a lime wedge.

Rum Collins
    1½ oz. rum
    Collins mix to fill
Garnish with a cherry and an orange slice. (You'll find a more elaborate recipe for Collinses in the Shaken Cocktails section, on page 62.)

Rum and Orange Juice
    1½ oz. rum
    orange juice to fill
Sometimes called a rum screwdriver.

Rum and Pineapple Juice
    1½ oz. rum
    pineapple juice to fill

Rum and 7-Up, Sprite, or Fruit Soda
1½ oz. vodka
7-Up, Sprite, or fruit soda to fill
Garnish with a lime wedge.

WHISKEY

The following highballs can contain bourbon, blended whiskey, Scotch, or some other whiskey. The drinker will tell the bartender what to put in—for example, Scotch and water. Often with these dark alcohols, drinkers prefer to choose a brand also—for example, a Dewar's and soda instead of just Scotch and soda.

Dealing with the many different kinds of whiskey often frustrates and confuses new bartenders, or even a drinker of light alcohols for that matter. If you fit into either of these categories, read over the whiskey section of Chapter 5 before trying to serve these drinks.

Whiskey and Water
1½ oz. whiskey
water to fill
Garnish with a lemon twist. Some people request only a splash of water. A splash equals ½ ounce, so just put a little water in (no need to measure) and serve it in a rocks glass.

Whiskey and Soda
1½ oz. whiskey
soda to fill
Garnish with a lemon twist.

Whiskey and Ginger
1½ oz. whiskey
ginger ale to fill
Some drinkers mean this when they ask for a "highball."

Presbyterian

 1½ oz. whiskey (usually blended)
 equal parts soda water and ginger ale to fill

This drink is often called a "Press" or a "VO Press." The latter contains Seagram's VO whiskey, a name brand. If you don't have VO, suggest another blended whiskey as a substitute.

John Collins

 1½ oz. whiskey
 Collins mix to fill

Garnish with a cherry and an orange slice. (You'll find a more elaborate recipe for Collinses in the Shaken Cocktails section, on page 62.)

Seven and Seven

 1½ oz. Seagram's 7
 7-Up to fill

This drink requires name-brand whiskey and the right mixer. If you don't have one or either, suggest substitutes. However, be sure to let the drinker know you are substituting ingredients.

Some whiskey drinkers want nothing to do with mixers. They'll order a Scotch on the rocks or blended whiskey with just a splash of water. Some will request a brand, such as "J&B neat." Serve these drinks in rocks glasses.

The garnish for dark alcohols is usually a lemon twist, both for lowballs (rocks) and highballs. With sweet mixers, leave out the twist.

Popular Highballs

The popular-drink section contains recipes that are either simple variations of the basics, or more complicated yet often ordered drinks. If you plan to work at a bar, memorize these recipes. They are arranged by liquor type (and, within these, by variations) to make it easier for you to remember ingredients and proportions.

Vodka and Apple Juice (or Lemonade)
    1½ oz. vodka
    apple juice or lemonade to fill

Downeaster
    1½ oz. vodka
    equal amounts of pineapple juice and cranberry juice to fill

Moscow Mule
    1½ oz. vodka
    ginger beer to fill
Garnish with a lime wedge. Traditionally served in a copper mug.

Harvey Wallbanger
    1½ oz. vodka
    orange juice (fill almost to top)
    1 oz. Galliano (float on top)
This is a screwdriver with Galliano on top.

Orange Chiller
    1½ oz. gin
    ginger ale to ¾ fill
    orange juice to fill
This is a gin chiller with some orange juice in it.

Rum Cape Codder
        1½ oz. rum
        cranberry juice to fill
Just substitute rum for the vodka in a Cape Codder.

Tequila Sunrise
        1½ oz. tequila
        orange juice to fill
        splash (½ oz.) of grenadine
Make this like a tequila screwdriver and stir. Then, gently add the grenadine to the top of the drink to achieve the sunrise look.

Claudio's Tequola
        1½ oz. tequila
        cola to fill
Garnish with a lime wedge. This is a tequila version of the Cuba libre. Drinkers call this by other names, such as tequila and cola.

Bloody Maria
> 1½ oz. tequila
> tomato juice to ¾ fill
> small splash lemon juice (or garnish with a lemon slice or lime wedge)
> dash Worcestershire sauce
> dash Tabasco sauce (more for a hotter drink)
> a shake of salt and pepper
> ¼ tsp. horseradish (optional)

Garnish with a celery stick. Ask if the drinker would like the drink hot, and then adjust the Tabasco accordingly. This drink is a Bloody Mary with tequila instead of vodka.

Fred Fud Pucker
> 1½ oz. tequila
> orange juice (fill almost to top)
> 1 oz. Galliano (float on top)

This drink is a tequila version of the Harvey Wallbanger.

Long Island Iced Tea
> 1 oz. gin
> 1 oz. vodka
> 1 oz. rum
> 1 oz. tequila
> splash sour mix
> splash Rose's lime juice
> cola to fill (after stirring)

Iced Teas are very popular these days. If made correctly, they taste like real iced tea—but *feel* different. In states with stringent alcohol laws, drinks with as much hard alcohol as in Iced Teas (4 oz. or more) are prohibited.

The following five drinks have been grouped together so you can learn them easily. They are all variations on the screwdriver.

Sloe Driver
> 1½ oz. sloe gin
> orange juice to fill

Comfortable Screw
> 1½ oz. Southern Comfort
> orange juice to fill

This one is easy to remember; the "Comfort" in the name indicates the presence of Southern Comfort.

Sloe Screw
> 1½ oz. vodka
> 1 oz. sloe gin
> orange juice to fill

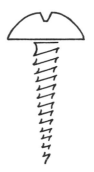

Sloe Comfortable Screw
> 1½ oz. vodka
> 1 oz. sloe gin
> 1 oz. Southern Comfort
> orange juice to fill

Sloe Comfortable Screw Up Against the Wall
> 1½ oz. vodka
> 1 oz. sloe gin
> 1 oz. Southern Comfort
> orange juice (almost to fill)
> 1 oz. Galliano (float on top)

These five drinks illustrate a helpful technique of how to remember drinks. Because so many drinks are simple variations on each other, look for key words in the name of the drink that give away the ingredients. A Sloe Comfortable Screw Up Against the Wall is an extremely complicated drink with many ingredients; however, by dissecting the title any rookie bartender should be able to make it: Sloe (sloe gin) Comfortable (Southern Comfort) Screw (vodka and orange juice) up against the wall (Galliano—as in a Harvey WALL banger).

Fun Highballs

You don't have to memorize these drinks because they aren't ordered too often, but keep this book at the bar just in case. They are listed alphabetically for easy reference.

Amaretto, Orange Juice, and Soda
>   1½ oz. amaretto
>   equal parts orange juice and soda to fill
Garnish with an orange slice.

Dark and Stormy
>   1½ oz. dark rum
>   ginger beer to fill
This delicious drink is popular in Bermuda, where they use Gosling's rum. If you can't find Gosling's, use another dark rum.

Gimlet Rickey
>   1½ oz. gin
>   1½ oz. Rose's lime juice
>   soda water to fill
Some people call this a "lime rickey."

Harvard Special
    1 oz. Galliano
    1½ oz. Pimm's No. 1
    ginger ale to fill
Garnish with an orange slice.

Kahlúa and Iced Coffee
    1½ oz. Kahlúa
    iced black coffee to fill

Kahlúa Root Beer Float
    1 oz. Kahlúa
    1 oz. root beer
    dash Galliano
    club soda to fill
    top with a scoop of vanilla ice cream
Do not serve on ice.

Kahlúa, Rum, and Soda
    1½ oz. Kahlúa
    1 oz. rum
    soda to fill

Mexicana
    1½ oz. tequila
    dash Rose's lime juice
    dash grenadine
    pineapple juice to fill

Orgasm
>   1½ oz. vodka
>   1½ oz. triple sec
>   splash Rose's lime juice
>   soda water, 7-Up, or Sprite to fill

This drink is similar to a Kamikaze, a shot drink. But it's much more fun to ask the bartender for an orgasm, isn't it?

Receptacle
>   1½ oz. vodka
>   splash each: orange, pineapple, cranberry juices
>   top with 7-Up or Sprite

Garnish with a cherry and an orange slice.

Very Screwy Driver
>   1 oz. vodka
>   1 oz. gin
>   1 oz. tequila
>   orange juice to fill

Garnish with a cherry and an orange slice.

Yellowbird
>   1½ oz. rum
>   ½ oz. triple sec
>   orange juice to fill

Garnish with a cherry and an orange slice.

Stirred Cocktails

A stirred cocktail contains about 3 to 4 ounces of liquid and is served in a cocktail glass for a straight-up drink or in a rocks glass for an on-the-rocks drink. The exact amount of liquid in the drink depends on the size of the serving glass. Just remember to keep the proportions the same as listed in these recipes, and don't be afraid to eyeball it if you need to. Ask if the drinker prefers a "rocks" or "up" drink, and then:

1. Fill a 12-ounce shaker glass two-thirds full with ice.
2. Put smallest ingredient in first until all ingredients are in the shaker.
3. Stir well.
4. Strain the drink into serving glass.
5. Garnish, if necessary.

Basic Stirred Cocktails

Memorize these classics. Unless you work at a fancy bar, you probably won't make very many of these, but when you do they must be *perfect*. Martini drinkers are the fussiest people in the world. Be prepared.

MARTINIS

Martini
    1 part dry vermouth
    6–8 parts gin
Pour just a small splash of vermouth (about ½ an ounce or a one-count) in the shaker and then a five-count (2½ oz.) of gin. (Melted ice brings the liquid content up to 3 ounces.) Garnish with two olives (pitted and without pimentos).

Dry Martini
    1 part dry vermouth
    10–12 parts gin
Pour a quick dash of vermouth into the shaker, and then add a six-count (3 oz.) of gin. With such a high gin/vermouth ratio, it is impossible to eyeball proportions as recommended for other stirred cocktails. Garnish with two olives (pitted and without pimentos).

Extra-Extra-Dry Martini
    3 oz. gin

Pour a six-count (3 oz.) of gin into a shaker, strain into a cocktail glass, and don't let the vermouth bottle anywhere near the gin! Garnish with two olives (pitted and without pimentos).

> By now, you've probably noticed that the way to dry out a martini is to reduce the amount of vermouth in the drink. The extra-extra-dry martini is a frequently ordered drink—it sounds a lot more interesting than "a glass of cold gin." You may come up with your own method of minimizing the amount of vermouth.

Here are some martini variations:

Fifty-Fifty
    1 part dry vermouth
    1 part gin

Pour in about a three-count (1½ oz.) of vermouth and then eyeball as much gin. Or, for advanced bartenders, pour both at the same time, for a three-count. Garnish with two olives.

Gibson
    ½ oz. dry vermouth
    2½ oz. gin

A Gibson is a martini garnished with a cocktail onion.

Vodka Martini
    ½ oz. dry vermouth
    2½ oz. vodka

Substitute vodka for the gin in a martini. Reduce the vermouth for a dry drink.

Tequini or Tequila Martini
    ½ oz. dry vermouth
    2½ oz. tequila
Substitute tequila for the gin in a martini. Garnish with an olive and a lemon twist.

MANHATTANS

Manhattan
    ¾ oz. sweet vermouth
    3 oz. blended whiskey
    dash of bitters (optional—ask the drinker)
Garnish with a cherry. Notice that a Manhattan requires sweet vermouth, whereas a martini contains dry vermouth.

Dry Manhattan
    ¾ oz. dry vermouth
    3 oz. blended whiskey
    dash bitters (optional)
Garnish with a cherry. For the dry martini, reduce the amount of vermouth in the drink, but in a dry Manhattan, change the kind of vermouth from sweet to dry.

Perfect Manhattan
    ½ oz. sweet vermouth
    ½ oz. dry vermouth
    3 oz. blended whiskey
    dash of bitters (optional)
Garnish with a cherry.

Here are some Manhattan variations:

Rum Manhattan
    ¾ oz. sweet vermouth
    3 oz. rum
Substitute rum for the blended whiskey in a Manhattan. Garnish with a cherry.

Tequila Manhattan

¾ oz. sweet vermouth

3 oz. tequila

Substitute tequila for the blended whiskey in a Manhattan. Garnish with a cherry and a lime wedge.

Rob Roy

¾ oz. sweet vermouth

3 oz. Scotch

Substitute Scotch for the blended whiskey in a Manhattan. Garnish with a cherry.

Comfort Manhattan

¾ oz. sweet vermouth

3 oz. Southern Comfort

Substitute Southern Comfort for the blended whiskey in a Manhattan. Garnish with a cherry.

GIMLETS

Gimlet

¾ oz. Rose's lime juice

3 oz. gin

Serve in a cocktail glass.

Vodka Gimlet

¾ oz. Rose's lime juice

3 oz. vodka

Substitute vodka for the gin in a gimlet.

STINGERS

Stinger

2 oz. five-star brandy

2 oz. white crème de menthe

To make a sweeter stinger, decrease the amount of brandy and increase the amount of crème de menthe.

To memorize stinger ingredients, think of the *stinging,* cool flavor of crème de menthe. Also, remember that the brandy bottle usually stands next to the crème de menthe on the back bar, so the two may be quickly picked up.

Vodka Stinger/Scotch Stinger/Amaretto Stinger/Galliano Stinger
    2 oz. appropriate liquor
    2 oz. white crème de menthe
Substitute the liquor of your choice for the five-star brandy in a stinger.

International Stinger
    1 oz. Galliano
    1 oz. Metaxa
    2 oz. white crème de menthe

The following drinks are similar to stingers:

Mocha Mint
    1 oz. Kahlúa or coffee brandy
    1 oz. white crème de cacao
    1 oz. white crème de menthe

Peppermint Pattie
    1½ oz. dark crème de cacao
    1½ oz. white crème de menthe
Peppermint patties are brown on the outside, so use brown crème de cacao.

Flying Tiger
   1 oz. Galliano
   1 oz. vodka
   1 oz. white crème de menthe
This is a Galliano stinger with vodka.

OLD FASHIONEDS AND JULEPS

Old Fashioneds are prepared differently from other stirred cocktails:

1. Put ½ teaspoon of fine-grained sugar in the bottom of an Old Fashioned or other lowball glass. That little bump on the bottom of the Old Fashioned glass is there to remind you to do this.
2. Add a dash or two of bitters to the sugar.
3. Put a handful of ice cubes in the glass.
4. Pour in 2½ ounces of bourbon (a five-count).
5. Add a splash of water or soda water.
6. Garnish with a cherry, an orange slice, and a lemon twist.

Because of the carbonated soda water, there is no need to stir.

Tequila Old Fashioned/Rum Old Fashioned
Substitute appropriate liquor for the bourbon in a regular Old Fashioned.

Mint Julep
Make this drink exactly like the Old Fashioned, but leave out the bitters. Instead,
garnish with a mint sprig. This drink is
very popular in the South. It is the
traditional drink of celebration for the
Kentucky Derby.

Brandy Julep
Substitute five-star brandy for bourbon in a mint julep.

Popular Stirred Cocktails

Although they aren't classics, you'll get many requests for
these drinks in a professional bar, so you should memorize
them. Now for the good news—drinkers usually prefer these
on the rocks, so you can mix them right in the glass (a rocks
glass) rather than wasting time transferring them from a
shaker glass. The recipes are arranged according to common
ingredients and variations, to help you memorize.

Black Russian
> 2 oz. vodka
> 1 oz. Kahlúa

Mudslide
> 1 oz. Kahlúa
> 1 oz. Bailey's Irish Cream
> 1 oz. vodka

This is similar to a Black Russian, but with the addition of
Bailey's Irish Cream. Make sure to stir this drink well because
cream does not mix readily.

Brave Bull
> 2 oz. tequila
> 2 oz. Kahlúa

Iguana
> 1 oz. tequila
> 1 oz. Kahlúa
> 1 oz. vodka

An Iguana is similar to a Brave Bull, but with the addition of vodka.

Kahlúa and Amaretto
> 2 oz. Kahlúa
> 2 oz. amaretto

Black Watch
> 1½ oz. Kahlúa
> 1½ oz. Scotch
> splash of soda

Garnish with a lemon twist.

The Godfather
> 3 oz. whiskey
> 1 oz. amaretto

The Godmother
Substitute vodka for the whiskey in a Godfather.

Rusty Nail
> 2 oz. Scotch
> 2 oz. Drambuie

B and B
> 2 oz. brandy
> 2 oz. Benedictine

Fun Stirred Cocktails

You won't get many requests for these drinks, but they're here in case you need them. Recipes are arranged alphabetically in this section.

Blanche
> 1 oz. anisette
> 1 oz. triple sec
> 1 oz. curaçao

Bombay Cocktail
> 1 oz. brandy
> 1 oz. curaçao
> ½ oz. dry vermouth
> ½ oz. sweet vermouth

Garnish with a lemon twist.

Cool Whisper
> 2 oz. Scotch
> ½ oz. dry vermouth
> ½ oz. sweet vermouth

Garnish with a lemon twist.

Dubonnet Cocktail
> 1½ oz. Dubonnet
> 1½ oz. gin

Garnish with a lemon twist.

Flying Grasshopper
> 1 oz. green crème de menthe
> 1 oz. white crème de cacao
> 1 oz. vodka

This is similar to the Grasshopper, a shaken drink, but has vodka instead of cream.

French Breeze
>   2 oz. Pernod
>   1 oz. peppermint schnapps

Golden Glow
>   1 oz. Galliano
>   1 oz. Drambuie
>   1 oz. gin

The word "golden" is your tip that this drink contains Galliano.

Jelly Bean
>   1½ oz. five-star brandy
>   ½ oz. anisette

Kahlúa and Brandy
>   1½ oz. Kahlúa
>   1½ oz. brandy

Latin Manhattan
>   1 oz. rum
>   1 oz. dry vermouth
>   1 oz. sweet vermouth
>   2 dashes bitters (optional)

Garnish with a lemon twist.

Negroni
>   1 oz. gin
>   1 oz. Campari
>   1 oz. vermouth (either sweet or dry)

Saint Pat
>   1 oz. green crème de menthe
>   1 oz. Chartreuse
>   1 oz. Irish whiskey

Sazerac
2 oz. bourbon
1 tsp. sugar
dash bitters
dash Pernod
Garnish with a lemon twist.

Spanish Moss
1 oz. Kahlúa
1 oz. tequila
1 oz. green crème de menthe

Wandering Minstrel
1 oz. vodka
½ oz. Kahlúa
¾ oz. five-star brandy
¾ oz. white crème de menthe

Yale
1½ oz. gin
½ oz. dry vermouth
dash Crème Yvette
dash bitters (optional)

Shaken Cocktails

If you need to refresh your memory of how to make shaken drinks, review pages 27–31. Follow the procedure given there for all the basic shaken drinks and for all other shaken drinks served straight up. Later, you'll read about a shortcut suitable for some drinks.

The recipes in the first two sections are arranged in groups of similar drinks, in order to make them easier to master. You may find these recipes easy to remember, and then forge ahead into the real world only to encounter a new problem: you've memorized ingredients and proportions, but forgotten whether to shake or to stir! As a general rule, *shake fruit juice, sour mix, sugar, egg, and cream drinks, or drinks that contain other difficult-to-mix ingredients.* Some of the multi-liqueur drinks in the stirred section might actually mix better when shaken.

Many of these recipes call for sour mix, a concoction made with juice from one half lemon and a teaspoon of sugar. This ratio may be adjusted to your personal preference, but it is a good idea always to have a bottle of sour mix on hand when tending bar; it will save you a lot of time when making shaken drinks.

Basic Shaken Cocktails

SOURS

Whiskey Sour
> 2 oz. bourbon or blended whiskey
> 1 oz. sour mix
Garnish with a cherry and an orange slice.

Ward Eight
> 2 oz. bourbon or blended whiskey
> 1 oz. sour mix
> ½ oz. grenadine
Garnish with a cherry and an orange slice.

Other sour variations: Substitute rum, vodka, gin, tequila, apricot brandy, or Southern Comfort for the whiskey in a regular whiskey sour.

Scotch Sour
> 2 oz. Scotch
> juice of ½ lime
> 1 tsp. sugar

Garnish with a cherry and an orange slice. This recipe calls for lime juice instead of lemon, so you cannot use sour mix in this drink.

THE DAIQUIRI AND SOME VARIATIONS

Daiquiri
> 2 oz. rum
> juice of ½ lime
> 1 tsp. sugar

A daiquiri contains lime juice, not lemon, so you cannot use sour mix in it. Some bars stock a pre-mixed lime and sugar mixture (such as Quik-Lime), but it is not very common. In a crowded, busy bar, some bartenders make daiquiris with sour mix (like a rum sour) and then squeeze a couple of lime wedges on the top to fool the customer's taste buds.

Bacardi Cocktail
> 2 oz. Bacardi rum
> juice of ½ lime
> 1 tsp. sugar
> ½ oz. grenadine

Mai Tai
      2 oz. rum
      juice of ½ lime
      1 tsp. sugar
      ½ oz. grenadine
      ½ oz. orgeat (almond syrup)
      1 oz. curaçao
Garnish with a cherry and a pineapple slice.

THE MARGARITA

Margarita
      2 oz. tequila
      ½ oz. triple sec
      juice of ½ lime
Shake and strain into a salt-rimmed cocktail or champagne glass.

COLLINSES

Tom Collins
      2 oz. gin
      1 oz. sour mix
      soda water to fill
Shake gin and sour mix, strain into Collins glass, and top with soda water. Garnish with a cherry and an orange slice.

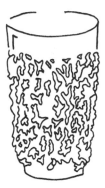

The main difference between a whiskey sour and a Collins is the addition of soda water, which carbonates the Collins. Also, the sour is usually served without ice in a sour glass, whereas the Collins goes over ice into a highball-like, frosted Collins glass.

The following drinks—the Singapore sling, sloe gin fizz, vodka Collins, John Collins, rum Collins and tequila Collins—are all similar to the Tom Collins. If you learn just their changes, it will be easier to remember how to make these drinks.

Singapore Sling

    2 oz. gin
    ½ oz. wild cherry brandy
    1 oz. sour mix
    soda water to fill

Shake gin, cherry brandy, and sour mix, strain into Collins glass, and top with soda water. Garnish with a cherry and an orange slice. This drink is a Tom Collins plus wild cherry brandy.

Sloe Gin Fizz.
>   2 oz. sloe gin
>   1 oz. sour mix
>   soda water to fill

Shake sloe gin and sour mix, strain into Collins glass with ice, and top with soda water. Garnish with a cherry and an orange slice. This is a Tom Collins with sloe gin substituted for gin.

John Collins
Substitute whiskey for the gin in a Tom Collins.

Vodka Collins/Rum Collins/Tequila Collins
Substitute the appropriate liquor for the gin in a Tom Collins.

That's it for the basic shaken drinks. If you think about it, they are all variations on four drinks: sours, daiquiris, margaritas, and Collinses. Try to remember the slight variations that distinguish each drink, as outlined below, and you should have no problem remembering everything in this section.

1. Whiskey Sour
   a. Ward Eight: add grenadine
   b. Scotch Sour: substitute Scotch for bourbon and lime juice for lemon juice
   c. Rum Sour
   d. Gin Sour
   e. Vodka Sour   } substitute appropriate liquor
   f. Tequila Sour
   g. Apricot Sour
   h. (Southern) Comfort Sour
2. Daiquiri
   a. Bacardi: add grenadine
   b. Mai Tai: add grenadine, orgeat, curaçao, and garnishes
3. Margarita

4. Tom Collins
   a. Singapore Sling: add wild cherry brandy
   b. Sloe Gin Fizz: substitute sloe gin for gin
   c. John Collins: substitute whiskey for gin
   d. Vodka Collins
   e. Rum Collins ⎫ substitute appropriate
   f. Tequila Collins ⎭ liquor

Popular Shaken Cocktails

Some of these drinks have become so popular in recent years that they're practically basics, so do memorize them if you plan to work in a bar some day. If you tend bar in a busy place, the whole shaker routine may become tiresome and begin to slow you down. To gain a little extra speed, use a half-shell shaker to short-shake drinks on the rocks. This gadget is a small, usually plastic shaker shell that fits over regular rocks and highball glasses. If you're using disposable plastic glasses, mix the drink in a highball glass and use a lowball glass for the half-shell.

Here are the steps for short-shaking:

1. Pour the drink ingredients over ice in the appropriate glass.
2. Fit the short-shaker securely over the glass.
3. Shake it up and down a few times.
4. Remove the shaker.

Quick and simple! This method is not as neat and thorough as the regular shaker technique, and *cannot* be used for straight-up cocktails, but it saves valuable time when you're in a hurry.

These drinks are arranged according to similar ingredients, to help you memorize.

Sombrero
1½ oz. coffee brandy
milk or cream to fill

Serve over ice in a rocks glass. Some bartenders prefer not to shake their Sombreros, the idea being that the cream floats on top like a hat.

Kahlúa Sombrero
Substitute Kahlúa for the coffee brandy in a Sombrero.

Italian Sombrero
Substitute amaretto for the coffee brandy in a Sombrero.

Amaretto and Cream
1½ oz. amaretto
1½ oz. cream

Serve in a rocks or cocktail glass.

Toasted Almond
1½ oz. Kahlúa or coffee brandy
1½ oz. amaretto
milk or cream to fill

Serve over ice in a rocks or highball glass.

Roasted Toasted Almond
Add 1½ oz. vodka to a Toasted Almond.

Creamsicle
1½ oz. amaretto
1½ oz. orange juice
milk or cream to fill

Usually served over ice in a rocks or highball glass. This drink tastes like the ice cream bar.

White Russian
2 oz. vodka
1 oz. Kahlúa or coffee brandy
½ oz. cream

Serve in a rocks glass. This drink, without the cream, is a Black Russian (a stirred drink).

Dirty Bird
An unstirred, unshaken White Russian.

Raz-Ma-Tazz
1½ oz. Kahlúa
1½ oz. Chambord
milk or cream to fill

Grasshopper
1 oz. green crème de menthe
1 oz. white crème de cacao
1 oz. cream

Serve in a rocks or cocktail glass (usually cocktail).

Mexican Grasshopper
Substitute Kahlúa for white crème de cacao in a Grasshopper.

Vodka Grasshopper
> ¾ oz. green crème de menthe
> ¾ oz. white crème de cacao
> ¾ oz. vodka
> ¾ oz. cream

Serve in a rocks or cocktail glass.

Girl Scout Cookie
> 1 oz. dark crème de cacao
> 1 oz. white crème de menthe
> 1 oz. cream

This is a Grasshopper with the liqueurs' colors reversed. Girl Scout mint cookies have chocolate on the outside (like dark crème de cacao) and white mint cookie on the inside (like white crème de menthe and cream).

Alexander
> 1 oz. gin
> 1 oz. dark crème de cacao
> 1 oz. cream

Serve in a rocks or cocktail glass.

Brandy Alexander
Substitute five-star brandy for gin in an Alexander. Dust the top with nutmeg.

Pink Squirrel
> 1 oz. crème de noyaux
> 1 oz. white crème de cacao
> 1 oz. cream

Usually served straight up in a cocktail glass. Memorize these ingredients by remembering that crème de noyaux is red and when mixed with cream it becomes pink. Squirrels eat nuts; crème de noyaux is almond-flavored.

Banshee

    1 oz. crème de banane
    1 oz. white crème de cacao
    1 oz. cream

Usually served straight up in a cocktail glass. This drink is similar to a Pink Squirrel, but with crème de banane instead of crème de noyaux. (Banshee and banana have the same first syllable.)

Melonball

    2 oz. Midori
    1 oz. vodka
    orange or grapefruit juice to fill

Serve over ice in a highball glass.

Pearl Harbor

Substitute pineapple for orange or grapefruit juice in a Melonball.

Honolulu Hammer

    1½ oz. vodka
    ½ oz. amaretto
    dash grenadine
    splash pineapple juice

Usually served straight up in a cocktail or shot glass.

Alabama Slammer

    1 oz. Southern Comfort
    1 oz. vodka
    dash grenadine
    dash sour mix
    splash orange juice

Serve in a highball, cocktail, or shot glass. For a slightly stronger drink, substitute sloe gin for grenadine. Be sure to ask if the drinker wants a highball or a shot and then vary the amounts of the ingredients accordingly, maintaining an equal ratio between the Southern Comfort and the vodka.

Apricot Bomb

    1½ oz. apricot brandy
    2 oz. vodka
    1½ oz. triple sec
    2 oz. sour mix
Serve over ice in a highball glass.

Cherry Bomb

Substitute cherry brandy for apricot in an Apricot Bomb.

Scarlett O'Hara

    1½ oz. Southern Comfort
    1½ oz. cranberry juice
    juice of ½ lime
Think of Scarlett and remember that
scarlet cranberry juice gives the
drink its red color. Scarlett O'Hara
of *Gone With the Wind* reminds
most people of the South, so it
should be easy to remember the
Southern Comfort.

Zombie

    2 oz. rum
    1 oz. Jamaican rum
    ½ oz. apricot brandy
    1 oz. orange juice
    1 oz. pineapple juice
Shake and strain into a highball glass over fresh ice. Float on
top ½ oz. of 151-proof rum. Garnish with a pineapple slice
or chunk and a cherry. Serve with straws.

Zombie (variation)

    1 oz. light rum
    ½ oz. Jamaican rum
    ½ oz. crème de noyaux
    ½ oz. triple sec
    1 oz. lemon juice
    1 oz. orange juice

Shake, strain into a highball glass over fresh ice, and top with soda water. Garnish with a pineapple slice or chunk and a cherry.

Iced Tea

    1 oz. vodka
    1 oz. gin
    1 oz. tequila
    1 oz. triple sec
    splash of lemon juice

Shake, strain into a highball glass over fresh ice, and fill with cola. See page 44 for a slightly different recipe.

Planter's Punch

    2 oz. rum
    1 oz. Myers's rum (Jamaican)
    juice of 1 lime
    1 tsp. sugar

Shake, strain into a highball glass over fresh ice, and fill with soda water. Garnish with an orange slice and a cherry.

Planter's Punch (variation)

    2 oz. rum
    1 oz. sour mix
    splash orange juice
    splash pineapple juice

Shake, strain into a highball glass over fresh ice, then swirl on top ½ oz. Myers's rum (Jamaican) and ½ oz. curaçao. Garnish with cherry and orange slice. Serve with a straw. The liquors on top give the drink its "punch" when it is sipped through a straw. The drinker finishes the bottom part first and gets an extra boost from the rum and curaçao at the end.

> Those Planter's Punch recipes look tough to memorize, don't they? You're in luck—the Myers's rum bottle has a recipe printed right on the label, so you can cheat if necessary.

EGGNOGS

Standard Eggnog
    1 egg
    1 tsp. sugar
    1½ oz. liquor (brandy, whiskey, rum, or a combination)
    6 oz. milk
Shake with ice and strain into a highball glass without ice. Dust with nutmeg.

Fruity Eggnog
    1 egg
    ½ oz. triple sec
    2 oz. apricot brandy
    6 oz. milk
Shake with ice and strain into a highball glass without ice. Dust with nutmeg.

For an extrafoamy nog, try mixing these eggnogs in the blender. For an eggnog punch recipe, see page 117.

Fun Shaken Cocktails

Just glance through these drinks to see if they sound good, but don't worry about memorizing them. They are listed alphabetically for easy reference.

Between the Sheets

    1 oz. five-star brandy
    1 oz. triple sec
    1 oz. rum
Shake and strain into a cocktail glass.

Bullshot

    1½ oz. vodka
    4 oz. beef bouillon
    dash Worcestershire sauce
Shake without ice, strain into a highball glass with ice, and garnish with a lemon twist.

California Lemonade

    2 oz. blended whiskey
    1 oz. sour mix
    juice of 1 lime
    dash grenadine
Shake, strain into a Collins glass over fresh ice, and fill with soda water. Garnish with an orange slice, a lemon twist, and a cherry.

California Root Beer

    1½ oz. Kahlúa
    1½ oz. milk
    1 oz. Galliano
Shake in a highball glass, and fill with root beer.

Cherry Rum

    1½ oz. rum
    ½ oz. cherry brandy
    ½ oz. cream
Shake well and strain into a cocktail glass over ice.

Chocolate Daisy
    1½ oz. five-star brandy
    1½ oz. port wine
    1 oz. sour mix
    splash grenadine
Shake and strain into a cocktail glass over ice.

Chocolate Mint Rum
    1 oz. rum
    ½ oz. dark crème de cacao
    1 oz. white crème de menthe
    ½ oz. cream
Usually served on the rocks.

Chuckie
    1½ oz. vodka
    dash curaçao
    splash pineapple juice
    splash orange juice
Shake and strain into a rocks glass over fresh ice, and top with soda. Garnish with a cherry.

Cream Puff
    2 oz. rum
    1 oz. cream
    1 tsp. sugar
Shake and strain into a cocktail glass over fresh ice.

Creamy Mocha Mint
    ¾ oz. Kahlúa or coffee brandy
    ¾ oz. white crème de cacao
    ¾ oz. white crème de menthe
    ¾ oz. cream
Shake and strain into a rocks glass over fresh ice.

Cuban Special
    1 oz. rum
    dash triple sec
    splash pineapple juice
    juice of ½ lime
Shake and strain into a rocks glass over fresh ice. Garnish with a cherry.

Dirty Mother
    1½ oz. Kahlúa or coffee brandy
    1½ oz. tequila
    milk or cream to fill
Shake and strain into a rocks or highball glass over fresh ice.

Dirty Virgin
    2 oz. gin
    1 oz. dark crème de cacao
Shake and strain into a rocks glass over fresh ice.

El Presidente Herminio
    1½ oz. rum
    ½ oz crème de banane
    ½ oz. curaçao
    splash orange juice
    splash pineapple juice
Shake and strain into a lowball glass over fresh ice.

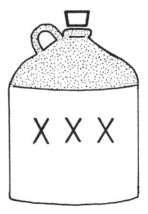

Fan

2 oz. Scotch
1 oz. triple sec or Cointreau
1 oz. grapefruit juice
Shake and strain into a rocks
glass over fresh ice.

Georgia Cream

1 oz. peach brandy
1 oz. White crème de cacao
1 oz. cream
Shake and strain into a rocks
glass over fresh ice.

Golden Apple

1 oz. Galliano
½ oz. applejack
½ oz. white crème de cacao
Shake and strain into a champagne
glass rimmed with maraschino
cherry juice and dipped in coconut powder.

Golden Cadillac

1 oz. Galliano
1 oz. white crème de cacao
1 oz. cream
Shake and strain into a rocks glass over fresh ice.

Golden Dream

1 oz. Galliano
½ oz. triple sec or Cointreau
½ oz. cream
1½ oz. orange juice
Shake and strain into a rocks glass over fresh ice.

Guana Grabber

    1 oz. light rum
    1 oz. dark rum
    1 oz. coconut rum (such as Malibu or Cocoribe)
    3 oz. pineapple juice
    1 oz. grapefruit juice
    dash grenadine
Shake and strain into a rocks glass over fresh ice.

Harvard

    1½ oz. five-star brandy
    ½ oz. dry vermouth
    1 tsp. grenadine
    juice of ½ lemon
Shake and strain into a rocks glass over fresh ice.

Jack Rose

    2 oz. applejack
    juice of ½ lemon
    1 tsp. grenadine
Shake and strain into a rocks glass over fresh ice.

Jamaican Cream

    1 oz. Jamaican rum
    1 oz. triple sec
    1 oz. cream
Shake and strain into a rocks glass over fresh ice.

James Bond 007

A vodka martini stirred, not shaken. (However, Bond once ordered bourbon, no ice.)

Kahlúa Cream Soda
1 oz. Kahlúa
4 oz. cream
Shake, strain into a highball glass over fresh ice, and fill with soda water.

Mocha Cream
1 oz. Kahlúa or coffee brandy
1 oz. white crème de cacao
1 oz. cream
Shake and strain into a rocks glass over fresh ice.

Pink Lady
2 oz. gin
1 oz. cream
½ oz. grenadine
1 egg white
Shake and strain into a cocktail glass.

Ramos Fizz
1½ oz. gin
juice of ½ lemon
juice of ½ lime
1½ oz. cream
½ tsp. sugar
1 egg white
Shake and strain into a rocks glass over fresh ice.

Red Russian
1 oz. strawberry liqueur
1 oz. vodka
1 oz. cream
Shake and strain into a rocks glass over fresh ice.

Russian Bear

   1 oz. vodka
   1 oz. dark crème de cacao
   1 oz. cream
Shake and strain into a rocks glass over fresh ice.

Sidecar

   1 oz. five-star brandy
   1 oz. triple sec
   juice of ½ lemon
Shake and strain into a cocktail glass.

Tam-o'-Shanter (Irish Sombrero)

   1 oz. Kahlúa or coffee brandy
   ½ oz. Irish whiskey
   milk to fill
Shake with ice in a highball glass.

Tootsie Roll

   1½ oz. Kahlúa
   1½ oz. dark crème de cacao
   orange juice to fill
Shake with ice in a highball glass. When made correctly, this
drink tastes like a Tootsie Roll.

Tropical Gold

   1 oz. rum or vodka
   ½ oz. crème de banane
   orange juice to fill
Shake with ice in a highball glass. Garnish with an orange slice
and a pineapple chunk.

Velvet Kiss

> 1 oz. gin
> ½ oz. crème de banane
> 1 oz. cream
> splash pineapple juice
> splash grenadine

Shake with ice in a highball glass.

The Latest and Greatest Drinks

Bartending is constantly changing. With so many new drinks appearing in bars across the country, it would be impossible to list them all. We've included a new section in our book, with a lot of drinks that may not have been around a few years ago. Don't feel that you need to memorize them all, but if you plan to work in a bar with a relatively young clientele, make sure you know what's in many of these drinks. These latest hits and a few of our personal favorites are arranged alphabetically for easy reference.

A.J.B.

> ½ oz. amaretto
> ½ oz. Jägermeister
> ½ oz. Bailey's Irish Cream

Shake well and strain into a shot glass. The unusual combination of ingredients gives this drink its name.

B-52

> ½ oz. Grand Marnier
> ½ oz. Bailey's Irish Cream
> ½ oz. Kahlúa

Serve straight up in a shot glass.

Blowjob

½ oz. vodka
½ oz. Tia Maria
½ oz. Kahlúa
small glob of whipped cream on top

This is served straight up in a shot glass. The drinker puts his/her mouth entirely over the shot glass and cranes the neck back to drink. No hands allowed!

Brain

¾ oz. Kahlúa
¾ oz. vodka
splash of Bailey's Irish Cream

Usually served straight up in a shot glass. It's the swirling of the Bailey's, which should be added last, that creates the "brain" texture.

Brain Hemorrhage

Add a splash of grenadine to a Brain. The red-colored grenadine swirls with the Bailey's to create the image that gives this drink its name.

Buffalo Sweat

¾ oz. Tabasco sauce
¾ oz. 151-proof rum
bar rag juice to fill

Serve straight up in a shot glass. This drink is a popular "rite-of-passage" drink especially suitable for twenty-first birthdays. Occasionally a customer will ask you to surprise them with something unusual, and a Buffalo Sweat is usually a good choice!

Cement Mixer
>1 oz. Bailey's Irish Cream
>1 oz. lime juice

The drinker leans his or her head back and the bartender pours a shot of each ingredient into the open mouth. The swirling effect of the ingredients coupled with its unusual method of consumption gives this drink its name.

Comfortable Pirate
>1½ oz. Captain Morgan's spiced rum
>1 oz. Southern Comfort
>pineapple juice to fill

Shake and strain into a highball glass over fresh ice.

Dead Nazi
>1 oz. Jägermeister
>1 oz. Rumple Minze peppermint
>schnapps

Serve straight up in a shot glass.

Grape Crush
>¾ oz. vodka
>¾ oz. Chambord
>splash sour mix

This latest trend is served straight up in a shot glass.

Hot Shot (also called a Fire Ball)
>¾ oz. cinnamon schnapps
>¾ oz. Tabasco sauce

Serve straight up in a shot glass.

Hummer
    1 oz. light rum
    ½ oz. Kahlúa
    1½ oz. cream
Shake well and serve straight up in
a cocktail glass.

Hurricane
    ¾ oz. Jägermeister
    ¾ oz. Yukon Jack
    splash of Bailey's Irish Cream
Do not shake or stir this shot. The Bailey's will create a swirling effect that gives this drink its name.

Jell-O Shots
    12 oz. vodka
    12 oz. water
    6 oz. Jell-O gelatin mix, flavor optional
Mix 6 ounces of vodka with 6 ounces of water and bring to a
boil. Stir in Jell-O gelatin mix. Remove from stove and add
remaining 6 ounces of water and 6 ounces of vodka. Let set
in refrigerator overnight.

    The "shots" can be semigelatinous and drinkable or
jelled and eaten with a spoon. Remove the mix from the refrigerator earlier if you do not want solidified Jell-O. The
drinker should be aware that because Jell-O shots are not
completely liquid the alcohol takes slightly longer to be absorbed into the bloodstream, delaying its effect. For more information on the physiology of alcohol absorption, see
Chapter 6.

Koolaid
1 oz. vodka
1 oz. Southern Comfort
1 oz. amaretto
1 oz. Midori
cranberry juice to fill
Serve with ice in a highball glass.

Lemon Drop
¾ oz. Absolut Citron
¾ oz. triple sec
Serve straight up in a shot glass. Give the drinker a lemon slice dipped in sugar as a chaser.

Mind Eraser
1½ oz. Kahlúa
1½ oz. vodka
7-Up, Sprite, or soda water to fill
Pour over ice in a highball glass and serve with a straw. Do not shake or stir, since the layering of ingredients is part of the effect. The drinker finishes it off like a shot "down in one" through the straw.

Orange Crush
¾ oz. vodka
¾ oz. triple sec
splash soda water
Serve straight up in a shot glass.

Oriental Rug
1 oz. Kahlúa
1 oz. Bailey's Irish Cream
1 oz. Frangelico
1 oz. Jägermeister
cola to fill
Serve over ice in a highball glass. The many colors swirling around give this drink its name.

Peanut Butter and Jelly (also called Nuts and Berries)
    ¾ oz. Frangelico
    ¾ oz. Chambord
Serve straight up in a shot glass.

Prairie Fire
    1.5 oz. tequila
    Tabasco sauce to fill
Serve straight up in a
shot glass.

Purple Haze
    1½ oz. vodka
    1½ oz. Chambord
    1 oz. triple sec
    splash of lime juice
    soda water to fill
Serve over ice in a highball glass. Like a Mind Eraser, this drink
is served in a highball glass, but the drinker finishes it off
"down in one" through a straw. This is a specialty of Preston's
at the Crimson Sports Grille in Cambridge.

Red Death
Splashes of vodka, sloe gin, Southern Comfort, amaretto, triple sec, lime juice, and orange juice. Add some sour mix for
flavoring and enough grenadine for a deep red color. This
nasty concoction is usually served as a shot.

Ren and Stimpy
    1½ oz. gin
    1½ oz. Chambord
    diet (or regular) cola to fill
Garnish with a lime wedge and serve over ice in a highball
glass. This is a specialty of Pat's at Casablanca's in Cambridge.

Robitussin
    1 part Southern Comfort
    1 part amaretto
    splash grenadine
Serve straight up in a shot glass. This drink, when made correctly, tastes like that cough syrup your parents made you drink.

Sex on the Beach
    1½ oz. vodka
    1 oz. peach schnapps
    cranberry juice to ¾ full
    orange juice to fill
Serve with ice in a highball glass.

Sleazy Sex on the Beach
    1½ oz. vodka
    1 oz. Grand Marnier
    cranberry juice to ¾ full
    orange juice to fill
Serve with ice in a highball glass.

Snakebite
    1½ oz. Yukon Jack
    juice of ½ lime
Serve straight up in a shot glass.

Terminator
    ½ oz. Jägermeister
    ½ oz. Bailey's Irish Cream
    ½ oz. Rumple Minze peppermint schnapps
    ½ oz. bourbon
Serve straight up in a shot glass.

Watermelon

    1 oz. Southern Comfort
    1 oz. amaretto
    orange juice to ¾ full
    pineapple juice to fill
    dash of grenadine
Serve over ice in a highball glass.

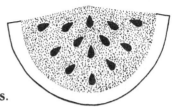

Windex

    ¾ oz. vodka
    ¾ oz. blue curaçao
Serve straight up in a shot glass.

There you have it, a partial list of some of the latest trends in bartending. You might have noticed that bars are beginning to serve more and more shots. Most of the bartenders we spoke to said they had noticed a trend away from mixed drinks and toward shots and beer.

Blended Drinks

Blended drinks (also called freezes or frozen drinks) taste incredibly delicious. Even the most stubborn and steadfast beer or whiskey drinkers have trouble refusing a frosty piña colada on a hot day!

To make blender drinks, follow these few simple steps:

1. Use only a heavy-duty blender.
2. With the motor off, mix the ingredients in the blender. Put the liquor in first, followed by mixers, then fruit, and finally ice (enough so the blender is three-quarters full).
3. Put the lid on.
4. Keeping fingers, hair, loose clothing, and small children at a safe distance, hold the lid down with one

hand and start the machine on low speed. After the initial mixing, change to high speed until the ingredients are well blended.

Most blenders range from 24 to 48 ounces in capacity. Since a typical highball glass holds about twelve ounces, adjust the ingredient amounts to fit your blender, while making sure you maintain the proportions of the original recipe.

In most recipes, the blender will be approximately three-quarters full. As with the ingredients, the exact amount of ice will vary, but simply eyeballing the right amount should be sufficient. In general, increasing the amount of ice in the blender will result in a thicker drink.

The following recipes are divided into five categories to help you memorize the ones you like: Coladas, Daiquiris, Margaritas, Tropical Drinks, and Ice Cream Drinks.

Coladas

Piña Colada
  2–3 oz. rum
  2–3 oz. coconut cream (comes in a can at the supermarket or liquor store)
  4–6 oz. pineapple juice
Blend with ice. Garnish with a cherry and a pineapple chunk. If you don't want to measure or use the amounts given in this recipe (in other words, if you just want to throw the ingredients in the blender any old way), follow this basic formula:

  as much rum as you want (1 part)
  1 part coconut cream
  2 parts pineapple juice

Hints:

- If you don't want a sweet piña colada, reduce the amount of coconut cream.
- For a slushy drink, add more ice.
- For a special touch, add a splash of grenadine and you'll have pink piñas.
- For a richer rum flavor, use golden or dark rum as well as light rum.

Midori Colada

>   2 oz. Midori
>   1 oz. rum
>   4 oz. pineapple juice
>   2 oz. coconut cream

Blend with ice. Garnish with a cherry, pineapple chunk, and/or melonball.

Daiquiris

Frozen Daiquiri

>   2 oz. rum
>   ½ oz. triple sec
>   1½ oz. lime juice
>   1 tsp. sugar

Blend with ice.

Banana Daiquiri

>   2 oz. rum
>   ½ oz. crème de cacao (either color)
>   ½ oz. crème de banane (optional)
>   1 sliced banana

Blend with ice.

Strawberry Daiquiri

>   2 oz. rum
>   ½ oz. strawberry liqueur (optional)
>   ½ cup fresh or frozen strawberries
>   1 tsp. sugar

Blend with ice.

Peach Daiquiri

Add to frozen daiquiri: 1 canned peach half with 1 oz. juice or ½ sliced fresh peach (more if desired). Optional: add ½ oz. peach-flavored brandy.

> You can keep adjusting the frozen daiquiri recipe for every fruit in the world. If you have a favorite fruit or flavoring, throw it into the blender with some rum, sour mix, and ice.

Margaritas

Margarita
2 oz. tequila
1 oz. triple sec
4 oz. lemon or lime juice
2 tsp. sugar

Blend with or without ice. Garnish with a lime slice (optional), and serve in a cocktail or champagne glass rimmed with salt.

> Always salt the rim before mixing the drink. To rim a glass with salt:
>
> 1. Cover a clean surface with a thin layer of rock salt.
> 2. Rub a lime wedge along the rim of the glass.
> 3. Turn the glass over and rub thoroughly in the salt.

Strawberry Margarita
2 oz. tequila
1 oz. triple sec
4 oz. lemon or lime juice
½ cup strawberries, fresh or frozen
1 oz. strawberry liqueur or 2 tsp. sugar

Blend with ice. Garnish with a fresh strawberry or a lime slice. Serve in a cocktail or champagne glass.

Midori Margarita

>   2 oz. tequila
>   1½ oz. Midori
>   1½ oz. sour mix

Blend with ice. Serve in a salted cocktail or champagne glass (salt optional).

Tropical Drinks

Tropical Storm

>   2 oz. rum (light, dark, or a mixture of both)
>   1 oz. crème de banane
>   ½ medium banana
>   4 oz. orange juice
>   dash grenadine

Blend with ice. Garnish with a cherry and an orange slice.

Scorpion

>   3 oz. light rum
>   ½ oz. brandy
>   2 oz. lemon juice
>   3 oz. orange juice

Blend with ice. Garnish with a cherry and an orange slice.

Blue Hawaiian
    2 oz. rum
    1 oz. blue curaçao
    1 oz. sour mix
    1 oz. orange juice
    1 oz. pineapple juice
Blend with ice.

Jump-Up-and-Kiss-Me
    2 oz. Galliano
    2 oz. rum
    ½ oz. apricot brandy
    juice of 1 lemon
    1 oz. pineapple juice
    2 egg whites
Blend with ice. Serve in a brandy snifter.

Ice Cream Drinks

Mississippi Mud
    1½ oz. Southern Comfort
    1½ oz. Kahlúa or coffee brandy
    2 scoops vanilla ice cream
Blend without ice. Garnish with chocolate shavings.

Hammer
    1 oz. Kahlúa or coffee brandy
    1 oz. light rum
    2 scoops vanilla ice cream
Blend without ice.

Blended White Russian
    1 oz. Kahlúa
    2 oz. vodka
    2 scoops vanilla ice cream
Blend without ice.

Coffee/Cocoa Brandy Alexander
1 oz. Kahlúa, coffee brandy, or crème de cacao
1 oz. brandy or cognac
2 scoops vanilla ice cream

Blend without ice.

Coffee Cacao Cream
½ cup crème de cacao
splash white crème de menthe
½ cup cold black coffee
1 scoop vanilla ice cream

Blend without ice.

Hot Drinks

There's nothing like a warm drink on a cold day, so here are a few of our favorites. Most of these drinks specify an ingredient or two to be added to a nonalcoholic hot drink such as coffee, cider, or tea. For mixing purposes, assume that the serving size of that drink is what you would drink normally— about 5 to 8 ounces. The drinks are listed alphabetically for easy reference.

Coffee Drinks

Amaretto Café
1½ oz. amaretto
hot black coffee

Stir. Top with whipped cream.

Café Mexicano
1 oz. Kahlúa
½ oz. tequila
hot black coffee

Stir. Garnish as desired.

Creamy Irish Coffee
1½ oz. Bailey's Irish Cream
hot black coffee
Stir. Top with whipped cream.

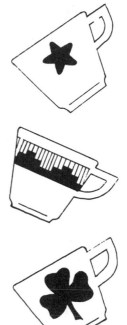

Irish Coffee
1½ oz. Irish whiskey
1 tsp. sugar
hot black coffee
Stir. Top with whipped cream.

Jamaican Coffee
1 oz. Tia Maria (or Kahlúa)
¾ oz. rum
hot black coffee
Stir. Top with whipped cream, if
desired, and dust with nutmeg.

Kahlúa Irish Coffee
1 oz. Kahlúa
1 oz. Irish whiskey or Bailey's Irish
Cream
hot black coffee
Stir. Garnish as desired.

Kioki Coffee
1 oz. Kahlúa
½ oz. brandy
hot black coffee
Stir. Garnish as desired.

Mexican Coffee
1½ oz. Kahlúa
hot black coffee
Stir. Top with whipped cream, if desired, and dust with nutmeg or add cinnamon stick.

Nutty Coffee
> 1 oz. amaretto
> ½ oz. Frangelico
> hot black coffee

Stir. Top with whipped cream.

Roman Coffee
> 1½ oz. Galliano
> hot black coffee

Stir. Top with whipped cream.

Other Hot Drinks

Chimney Fire
> 1½ oz. amaretto
> hot cider

Garnish with a cinnamon stick.

Chimney Fire Variations
Substitute Southern Comfort or dark rum for amaretto.

Comfort Mocha
> 1½ oz. Southern Comfort
> 1 tsp. instant cocoa or hot chocolate
> 1 tsp. instant coffee

Add boiling water. Top with whipped cream if desired.

Good Night
> 2 oz. rum
> 1 tsp. sugar
> warm milk

Serve in a mug. Dust with nutmeg.

Grog
    1½ oz. rum
    1 tsp. sugar
    juice of ¼ lemon
    boiling water
Serve in a mug.

Hot Buttered Rum
    2 oz. rum
    1 tsp. sugar
    1 tsp. butter
    boiling water
Dust with nutmeg.

Hot Italian
    2 oz. amaretto
    warm orange juice
Garnish with a cinnamon stick.

Hot Toddy
    2 oz. whiskey
    1 tsp. sugar
    boiling water
Serve in a mug. Garnish with lemon slice and dust with nutmeg or add cinnamon stick.

Hot Wine Lemonade
    1½ oz. red wine
    juice of ½–1 lemon
    1½ tsp. sugar
    boiling water
Garnish with a lemon twist.

Italian Tea
    1½ oz. amaretto
    1 tsp. sugar (optional)
    hot tea
Stir. Top with whipped cream.

Kahlúa and Hot Chocolate
    1 oz. Kahlúa
    hot chocolate
Top with whipped cream.

Tom and Jerry
Beat until stiff:
    1 egg white
    2 tsp. sugar
    pinch baking soda
    ½ oz. rum
Combine 1 tbsp. of this mixture with:
    2 tbsp. hot milk
    1½ oz. rum
Put mixture in a warm mug and fill with more hot milk. Float on top ½ oz. five-star brandy. Dust with nutmeg.

Flame Drinks

Flaming drinks can be a lot of fun when done safely and correctly. To flame a drink, first warm only one teaspoon of the required liquor over a match flame, then ignite. Once it is lit, *carefully* pour it over the prepared recipe. Stand back! This method is usually safer than lighting the liquor right in the glass.

Blue Blazer

  2½ oz. whiskey
  2½ oz. boiling water
  1 tbsp. honey (optional)

Pour the whiskey and the boiling water into two separate mugs. Ignite the whiskey. Mix by pouring back and forth several times between the two mugs. Garnish with a lemon twist and serve in a warm on-the-rocks glass. Add honey if desired.

  In a darkened room, the mixing process will look like you're pouring liquid, blue fire.

Southern Blazer

Substitute 1½ oz. Southern Comfort and 1 oz. Kahlúa for the whiskey in the Blue Blazer recipe. After mixing, add two dashes of bitters and garnish with an orange slice.

Brandy Blazer

  2 oz. five-star brandy
  1 tsp. sugar
  1 piece orange peel
  1 lemon twist

Put ingredients in an Old Fashioned or rocks glass. Ignite. Stir with bar spoon, then strain into a thick, stemmed glass.

Café Royale

  1 cube of sugar soaked in five-star brandy
  1 cup of hot black coffee

Ignite sugar in spoon and drop into coffee as it caramelizes and the flame dies out.

Flaming Harbor Light

In a shot glass, layer:

  ½ oz. Kahlúa
  ½ oz. tequila
  ½ oz. 151-proof rum

Ignite.

Lighthouse

2 oz. Galliano
2 oz. dry vermouth

Ignite Galliano in shot glass and pour it over dry vermouth in a cocktail glass. May be served on the rocks in a champagne glass and garnished with a lemon slice.

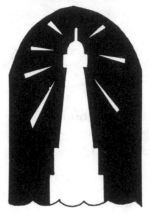

Pousse-Cafés

Pousse-cafés are layered drinks. When you pour several liquids carefully into a shot glass, the heaviest ones stay on the bottom and the lightest ones float to the top, thus creating layers.

To make a pousse-café, be careful! Move slowly. Pour each ingredient onto the bar spoon handle (that's why the bar spoon handle is twisted) and let it slide gently into the shot glass via the edge of the glass. Always pour the heaviest liquid first, then the next heaviest, and so on.

The recipes here list the ingredients from heaviest to lightest, so pour them in the order given. Pour just enough of each liquid to get a smooth, flat layer; however, feel free to experiment with the proportions listed here to change the thickness of the layers.

Angel's Delight
- 1 part grenadine
- 1 part triple sec
- 1 part Crème Yvette
- 1 part cream

Angel's Kiss
- 1 part white crème de cacao
- 1 part Crème Yvette
- 1 part five-star brandy
- 1 part cream

Angel's Tip
- 1 part brown crème de cacao
- 1 part cream

Stick a toothpick through a cherry and balance it on top of the glass.

Angel's Wing
- 1 part white crème de cacao
- 1 part five-star brandy
- 1 part cream

Christmas
- 1 part grenadine
- 2 parts green crème de menthe

Fifth Avenue
- 1 part dark crème de cacao
- 1 part apricot brandy
- 1 part cream

King Alphonse
An angel's tip without the cherry.

King's Cup
2 parts Galliano
1 part cream

Princess
3 parts apricot brandy
1 part cream

Stars and Stripes
1 part grenadine
1 part heavy cream
1 part Crème Yvette

Make Your Own Pousse-Cafés

Each liqueur has a specific weight. The key to making pousse-cafés is to put the heaviest liqueur in the glass first, then the next heaviest, and so on. Cream floats on the top. Technically, you could probably layer all of the liqueurs listed here on top of each other, but most pousse-cafés have only three to five layers.

The following chart assigns numbers to the relative weights of the most popular pousse-café liqueurs, from heaviest to lightest:

Liqueur	Relative Weight
Anisette (50 proof)	17.8
Crème de noyaux (50 proof)	17.7
Crème de menthe (60 proof)	15.9
Crème de banane (50 proof)	15.0
Maraschino liqueur (50 proof)	14.9
Coffee liqueur (50 proof)	14.2
Cherry liqueur (48 proof)	12.7
Parfait Amour (50 proof)	12.7
Blue curaçao (60 proof)	11.7
Blackberry liqueur (50 proof)	11.2

Apricot liqueur (58 proof)	10.0
Orange curaçao (60 proof)	9.8
Triple sec (60 proof)	9.8
Coffee brandy (70 proof)	9.0
Peach brandy (70 proof)	7.0
Cherry brandy (70 proof)	6.8
Blackberry brandy (70 proof)	6.7
Apricot brandy (70 proof)	6.6
Rock and Rye liqueur (60 proof)	6.5
Ginger brandy (70 proof)	6.1
Peppermint schnapps (60 proof)	5.2
Kummel (78 proof)	4.2
Peach liqueur (60 proof)	4.1
Sloe gin (60 proof)	4.0

Wine and Champagne Drinks

Wine Drinks

Kir
> dash crème de cassis
> dry white wine, chilled, to fill

Serve in a wine glass.

Spritzer
> 1 part white wine
> 1 part club soda

Serve on ice with a lemon twist in a large wineglass or tall frosted highball glass.

Vermouth Apéritif
Serve sweet vermouth on ice with a lemon twist.

Vermouth Half and Half

> 1 oz. sweet vermouth
> 1 oz. dry vermouth

Add ice, stir, strain into wineglass. Fill with soda water. Garnish with a lemon twist.

For more wine drink recipes, see the Coolers section of this chapter.

Champagne Drinks

Bubbling Mint

> ½ oz. green crème de menthe
> champagne to fill

Serve in champagne glass.

Caribbean Champagne

> splash rum
> splash crème de banane

Pour into champagne glass. Add champagne to fill. Garnish with a banana slice.

Champagne Cocktail

> glass of champagne
> 2 dashes bitters
> 1 tsp. sugar

Stir without ice. Garnish with an extralong spiral twist of lemon peel.

Champagne Fizz

> 2 oz. gin
> 1 oz. sour mix

Shake, strain into a highball glass with ice, and fill with champagne.

French 75

>   1 oz. gin
>   2 oz. sour mix

Shake in a shaker glass with ice and strain over fresh ice into a highball or Collins glass. Add champagne to fill. Garnish with an orange slice and a cherry.

Kir Royale

>   dash crème de cassis
>   chilled champagne to fill

Serve in a champagne glass.

Mimosa

>   1 part champagne
>   1 part orange juice
>   dash triple sec

Garnish with an orange slice.

Midori Mimosa

>   2 oz. Midori
>   2 tsp. lime juice
>   champagne to fill

Garnish with a lime wedge and strawberries (optional).

Coolers

Serve these drinks over ice in tall, frosty glasses. At a busy bar, if a customer orders a wine cooler or spritzer, just pour about 3 ounces of wine over ice in a tall glass and fill with soda water.

Wine and Champagne Coolers

Champagne Cooler
    1 oz. brandy
    1 oz. Cointreau or triple sec
    champagne to fill
Garnish with mint sprigs.

Country Club Cooler
    3 oz. dry vermouth
    1 tsp. grenadine
    soda water to fill

Pineapple Wine Cooler
    2½ oz. dry white wine
    2½ oz. pineapple juice
    soda water to fill
Garnish with lemon and orange twist (extralong spirals). As an option, add 1 oz. rum before you pour in the soda water.

Red Wine Cooler
    2 tsp. sugar syrup
    1 oz. orange juice
    red wine to ¾ full
    top with soda water

White Wine Cooler
    1 tsp. sugar syrup
    white wine to ¾ full
    top with soda water
Garnish with mint sprigs.

Liquor-Based Coolers

Apricot Cooler
>1½ oz. apricot brandy
>2 dashes grenadine
>7-Up or Sprite to fill

Boston Cooler
>2 oz. rum
>½ oz. sour mix
>soda or ginger ale to fill

Garnish with lemon twist (extralong spiral) and orange slice.
This is a fizzier version of the rum Collins.

Gin Cooler/Vodka Cooler
Substitute the appropriate liquor for rum in the Boston
Cooler.

Rum Cooler
>3 oz. rum
>½ oz. lemon juice
>3 oz. pineapple juice
>tonic water to fill

Scotch Cooler
>2 oz. Scotch
>splash crème de menthe
>soda water to fill

Garnish with mint sprigs.

Tequooler (Tequila Cooler)
>1½ oz. tequila
>juice of ½ lemon or lime
>tonic water or soda water to fill

Garnish with a lemon twist (extralong spiral).

Beer Drinks

Are you the kind of connoisseur whose favorite cocktail is a beer straight from the can? You'll be amazed at what you can do with your old standby.

Serve these drinks in a beer mug or Pilsner glass.

Black Velvet
1 part porter or stout
1 part champagne (extra dry)
Pour these carefully down the side of the glass to make two distinct layers. In all, 10 to 16 ounces.

Half-and-Half
1 part ale
1 part porter or stout
In all, 10 to 16 ounces.

Shandy Gaff
1 part beer
1 part ginger ale
In all, 10 to 16 ounces.

Boilermaker

Add a jigger of whiskey to a mug of beer. You can (a) drink the whiskey and chase it with the beer (boring), (b) pour the shot into the beer (better), or (c) drop the shot—glass and all—into the mug of beer and chug it all down quickly before it foams all over you. This is sometimes called a "depth charge."

Beer and whiskey, mighty risky!

Sneaky Pete

To a mug of beer, add a jigger of applejack.

Hop-Skip-and-Go-Naked

    1 oz. vodka
    1 oz. gin
    juice of ½ lime
    beer to fill

Serve over ice. To serve as a punch, measure the ingredients by the bottle and case.

Light and Nonalcoholic Drinks

Even without alcohol, many of these concoctions are very good indeed and should be an option at any party. As a responsible bartender, a nonalcoholic drink is a necessity that can be used not only to quench the thirst of nondrinkers, but may also be an integral tool when deciding to cut someone off. In the past few years, nonalcoholic beers and wines have become increasingly popular and are a definite plus to have around when bartending. The selection of these drinks is constantly increasing and gives nondrinkers and designated drivers even more alternatives to drinking.

The term "light alcoholic" in the heading warrants further explanation. Many mixers such as bitters and extracts may contain alcohol and great care should be taken in their use. Certain people may have strong physiological reactions to even the smallest amounts of alcohol, so a responsible bartender should be aware of exactly what is going into a "nonalcoholic" drink.

Beach Blanket Bingo
        4 oz. cranberry juice
        4 oz. grape juice
Garnish with a lime wedge and serve over ice in a highball glass.

Cardinal Punch
        2 quarts cranberry juice
        1 quart orange juice
        juice of 4 lemons
        8 bottles ginger ale
Add ginger ale just before serving over ice.

Cranberry Cooler
        2 oz. cranberry juice
        juice of ½ lime
        soda water to fill
Serve over ice in a highball glass.

Fritzer

 1 tsp. sugar
 2 dashes bitters
 soda water to fill

Garnish with a lemon twist. Please note that some bitters contain small amounts of alcohol and may be harmful to some nondrinkers.

Fruit Juice Combo

 1 cup tomato juice
 1 cup V-8 (or other vegetable juice)
 1 cup apple juice
 1 cup cranberry juice
 1 cup grapefruit juice
 1 cup lemonade
 1 cup orange juice
 1 cup pineapple juice
 8 drops Tabasco sauce

Garnish with a skewer of fresh pineapple, orange, and apple slices to stir with. Serve over ice in a highball glass. Makes 8 servings.

Grapeberry

 4 oz. cranberry juice
 4 oz. grapefruit juice

Garnish with a lime wedge. Serve in a highball glass over ice.

Innocent Passion

 4 oz. passionfruit juice
 splash cranberry juice
 splash orange juice
 juice of ½ lemon
 soda water to fill

Serve over ice in a highball glass.

Kentucky Derby
      1½ cups sugar
      2 cups cold water
      1 cup lemon juice
      2 quarts ginger ale
Garnish with lemon slices
and mint sprigs.

Lime Cola
      juice of ½ lime
      cola to fill
Serve over ice in a highball glass.

Long Island Tall Boy
      6 oz. can lemonade concentrate
      1 quart orange juice
Garnish with strawberries and lime slices. Makes 4–8 servings.

Mickey Mouse
      1 scoop vanilla ice cream
      cola to fill
Top with whipped cream and two cherries. Serve with straw
and long-handled spoon.

Pink Snowman
      1 cup orange juice
      1 10 oz. package frozen strawberries
      2 large scoops vanilla ice cream
Blend and serve with another scoop of vanilla ice cream.

Red Rooster Punch
    4 cups V-8 (or other vegetable juice)
    10 oz. ginger ale
    1 tbsp. lime juice
    1 tsp. Worcestershire sauce
    dash Tabasco sauce
Makes about 6 servings. For other punch recipes, see pages 115–27.

Roy Rogers
    dash grenadine
    cola to fill
Garnish with a cherry.

Shirley Temple
    dash grenadine
    7-Up or Sprite to fill
Garnish with a cherry.

Strawberry Angel
    1 pint fresh strawberries
    1 13½ oz. can sweetened condensed milk
Blend with ice and serve in lowball glasses.

Sunset
    3 cups V-8 (or other vegetable juice)
    ½ tsp. horseradish
    ½ tsp. Worcestershire sauce
Makes 4 servings.

Unfuzzy Navel

    4 oz. peach nectar
    4 oz. orange juice
    juice of ½ lemon
    dash grenadine

Shake and serve over fresh ice in a highball glass. Garnish with an orange slice.

Unreal Champagne

    1 cup sugar
    2 cups water
    2 cups grapefruit juice
    juice of 1 lemon
    2 (28 oz.) bottles of ginger ale
    dash grenadine

Add ginger ale just before serving. Serve in champagne glasses. Makes 15–20 servings.

Vanilla Cola

    splash of vanilla extract
    cola to fill

Serve over ice in a highball glass. Vanilla extract frequently contains a small amount of alcohol and may be harmful to some nondrinkers.

Virgin Colada

    4–6 oz. coconut cream
    4–6 oz. pineapple juice

Blend with ice. Garnish with a cherry and a pineapple chunk and serve in a highball glass.

Virgin Mary

> tomato juice to ¾ full
> small splash lemon juice
> dash Worcestershire sauce
> dash Tabasco (more for a hot drink)
> shake of salt and pepper
> ¼ tsp. horseradish (optional)

There are an infinite number of combinations of fruit juices that can create drinkable beverages. Also, many popular drinks can be converted to their "virgin" counterparts simply by eliminating the alcohol in them. Once again, don't be afraid to experiment—you just may invent a popular new drink.

Punch Recipes

So you're a little shy about pouring in public? Try some of these punch recipes so you can show off your new bartending abilities while still mixing in the privacy of your own home. All of the following recipes should be served from a punch bowl with a large block of ice in it, unless directions specify otherwise. For each serving, ladle about 4 ounces into a plastic lowball glass.

Brandy Punch

Mix:

> juice of 1 dozen lemons
> juice of 4 oranges

Add sugar to taste. Mix with:

> 1 cup grenadine
> 1 cup triple sec
> 2 liters five-star brandy
> 2 cups tea (optional)
> 1 quart soda water

Add soda water just before serving. Garnish with fruit. Yields 35–50 servings.

Buddha Punch

> 1 bottle Rhine wine
> ½ cup curaçao
> ½ cup rum
> 1 cup orange juice
> 1 quart soda water
> Angostura bitters to taste
> 1 bottle chilled champagne

Add champagne just before serving. Garnish with mint leaves and fruit slices. Note: One bottle of champagne usually equals 750 milliliters or 1 quart. Either size is acceptable. Yields 25–30 servings.

Canadian Fruit Punch

> 2 liters Canadian whiskey
> 12 oz. can frozen orange juice concentrate
> 12 oz. can frozen lemonade concentrate
> 12 oz. can frozen pineapple juice concentrate
> 1 cup simple syrup (page 19)
> 3 quarts strong iced tea

Garnish with fruit. Yields 65–75 servings.

Claret Punch

2 bottles claret (or a 1½ liter bottle)
½ cup curaçao
1 cup simple syrup (page 19)
1 cup lemon juice
1 pint orange juice
½ cup pineapple juice
2 quarts soda water

Add soda water just before serving. Yields about 40 servings.

Eggnog

1 lb. confectioners' sugar
12 eggs, separated
1 pint brandy
1 pint light rum
1½ quarts milk
1 pint heavy cream

Beat confectioners' sugar in with egg yolks. Stir in slowly: brandy, rum, milk, and cream. Chill. Then fold in stiffly beaten egg whites before serving. Do not serve with ice. Sprinkle nutmeg on top. Yields 45–65 servings.

Fish House Punch

1 liter rum
1 bottle brandy (750 ml.)
½ cup peach brandy

2–3 quarts cola, or another flavored soda, or lemonade

Add soda just before serving. Garnish with citrus fruits. Yields 25–35 servings.

French Cream Punch

1 cup amaretto
1 cup Kahlúa or coffee brandy
¼ cup triple sec
½ gallon softened vanilla ice cream

No ice. Mix well. Yields 15–20 servings.

Fruit Punch
      1 liter vodka
      1 bottle white wine
      2 (12 oz.) cans frozen fruit juice concentrate
      (pineapple, grapefruit, or orange)
      2 quarts soda water
Add soda water just before serving. Yields about
40 servings.

Gin Punch
      2 liters gin
      1 pint lemon juice
      2 cups cranberry juice cocktail
      1 quart orange juice
      ½ cup grenadine
      1 quart soda water
Add soda water just before serving. Garnish with sprigs of
mint. Yields about 45 servings.

Green Machine
      2 liters vodka
      1 (12 oz.) can frozen limeade concentrate
      ½ pint lemon sherbert
      ½ pint lime sherbert
Yields about 35 servings.

Hot Apple Rum Punch
      1 liter dark rum
      1 quart apple cider
      2 or 3 cinnamon sticks, broken
      1½ tbsp. butter
Heat in saucepan until almost boiling. Serve hot. Yields about
15 servings.

Hot Mulled Wine

        2 cups water
        2 cinnamon sticks, whole
        8 cloves
        peel of 1 lemon, cut into twists or into one long spiral
        ¼ cup simple syrup (page 19)
        2 bottles of dry red wine

Boil everything in large saucepan for 10 minutes. Add wine. Heat but do not allow to boil. Just before serving add a splash of cognac and a lemon slice to each glass. Serve hot. Yields 15–25 servings.

Oogie Pringle Punch

        1 liter rum
        1 quart pineapple juice
        1 quart cranberry juice

Garnish with lemon slices. Yields about 25 servings.

Party Punch

Boil for 5 minutes:

        2 cups sugar
        1 cup water

Add:

        2 cups concentrated fruit syrup
        1 cup lemon juice
        2 cups orange juice
        2 cups pineapple juice

Just before serving, add:

        2 bottles chilled champagne
        2 quarts ginger ale
        1 quart soda water

Yields about 55 servings.

Planter's Punch

      1 liter rum
      1 pint Jamaican rum (Myers's)
      1 pint fresh lime juice
      1 pint simple syrup (page 19)
      1 quart soda water

Add soda water just before serving. Garnish with orange slices and cherries. Yields about 30 servings.

Planter's Punch (variation)

      1 liter rum
      1 cup Jamaican rum (Myers's)
      1 cup curaçao (optional)
      1 pint lemon juice
      1 cup orange juice
      1 cup pineapple juice

Garnish with orange slices and cherries. Yields about 20 servings.

Red Wine Punch

      2 bottles dry red wine
      1 pint lemon juice
      1 cup simple syrup (page 19)
      1 cup raspberry syrup
      2 quarts soda water

Add soda water just before serving. Yields about 40 servings.

Rum Fruit Punch

      1½ liters rum
      ½ pineapple, sliced
      1 pint strawberries
      ¾ cup simple syrup (page 19)
      1 cup lemon juice
      2 cups pineapple juice

Chill for 2 hours. Just before serving, add:

      1 pint thinly sliced strawberries
      2 quarts soda water

Yields 40–50 servings.

Sangría

2 bottles rosé wine
1 cup rum
2 cups orange juice
2 cups pineapple juice
1 quart ginger ale
30 oz. can fruit cocktail
3 sliced oranges
Yields 35–40 servings.

Sangría Maria

Blend together:

1 jug hearty burgundy wine (1½ liters)
1 quart ginger ale

Cut into wedges, squeeze, and drop in:

4 oranges
2 lemons
2 peaches
any other fruits you wish to add

Let stand for at least 2 hours. Strain into punch bowl with ice. Garnish with lemon slices, orange slices, and cherries. Yields about 25 servings.

Narri's Sangría

This delicious recipe comes from the bar of Narri, a former manager of the Harvard Bartending Course. Soak cut-up fruit (strawberries, oranges, lemons, limes, and whatever you like) overnight in:

2 cups dark rum

Add:

1 quart sweet red wine
1 quart dry red wine

Yields 25–30 servings.

Southern Comfort Punch
    1 bottle Southern Comfort (750 ml.)
    2 cups grapefruit juice
    1 cup lemon juice
    2 quarts 7-Up, Sprite, or ginger ale
Yields about 30 servings.

Sparkling Pink Punch
    1 bottle chilled champagne
    1 bottle rosé wine
Pour over:
    1 (10 oz.) container thawed whole frozen raspberries or
    strawberries
Yields about 15 servings.

Tequila Punch
    1 liter tequila
    4 bottles sauterne
    2 quarts fruit cubes and balls (8 cups)
    1 bottle chilled champagne
Sweeten to taste. Add champagne just before serving. Yields
about 45 servings.

Tropical Punch
Blend, cover, and let stand overnight:
    5 bottles white wine
    1 lb. brown sugar
    1 quart orange juice
    1 pint lemon juice
    5 sliced bananas
    1 pineapple, cut or chopped

Add:
    3 liters light rum
    1 pint dark rum
    2 cups crème de banane
    Strain into a punch bowl with ice. Garnish with fruits.
Yields about 100 servings.

Velvet Hammer Punch
    1 bottle sauterne
    12 ounces apricot brandy
    1 liter vodka
    1 bottle chilled champagne
    1 quart ginger ale
Add champagne and ginger ale just before serving. Yields about 30 servings.

Wedding Punch
    1 liter vodka
    3 cups orange juice
    1 cup lemon juice
    2 quarts ginger ale
Garnish with cherries, lemons, and orange slices. Yields about 35 servings.

Welder's Punch
    1 liter vodka
    1 quart ginger ale, 7-Up, or Sprite
    1 quart fruit punch
    1 quart orange juice
Garnish with orange slices and cherries. Yields about 35 servings.

Whiskey Punch
    2 liters bourbon
    ½ cup curaçao
    1 quart apple juice
    juice of 6 lemons
    2 ounces grenadine
    4 quarts ginger ale
Add ginger ale just before serving, garnish with cherries. Yields 60–65 servings.

Wine Punch

Dissolve:

>   1½ lbs. sugar

in:

>   2 quarts soda water

Add:

>   2 bottles dry red wine
>   1 pint brandy
>   1 pint rum

Before serving, add:

>   1 bottle sparkling white wine

Garnish with sliced oranges and pineapple slices. Yields 45–50 servings.

Champagne Punches

Champagne Punch

>   2 or 3 bottles chilled champagne
>   ½ cup curaçao
>   ½ cup lemon juice
>   1 quart soda water
>   ½ lb. confectioners' sugar

Mix this punch just before serving. Yields 25–35 servings.

Champagne Punch (variation)

>   ½ cup brandy
>   ½ cup Cointreau or triple sec
>   2 bottles chilled champagne

Yields about 15 servings.

Champagne Punch (variation)
½ cup light rum
½ cup dark rum
juice of 2 lemons
juice of 2 oranges
1 cup pineapple juice
½ cup sugar
2 bottles chilled champagne
Add champagne just before serving. Yields about 20 servings.

Champagne Punch (variation)
Slice and arrange 6 oranges on the bottom of a punch bowl. Sprinkle with sugar and add:
1 bottle Moselle wine
Let stand for at least one hour. Just before serving, place ice block in bowl and add 4 bottles chilled champagne. Yields about 30 servings.

Champagne Holiday Punch
1 bottle chilled champagne
2 quarts ginger ale
1 (8 oz.) can crushed pineapple with juice
1 quart raspberry sherbert
Mix this punch just before serving. Yields 25–35 servings.

Champagne Rum Punch
2 liters rum
1 bottle sweet vermouth (750 ml.)
1 quart orange juice
1 bottle chilled champagne
Add champagne just before serving. Garnish with sliced bananas. Yields about 40 servings.

Champagne Sherbert Punch
     1 quart lemon or pineapple sherbert
     2 bottles chilled champagne
     1 bottle sauterne

Put sherbert in first. Garnish with lemon slices and/or pineapple chunks. Yields about 25 servings.

Nonalcoholic Punches

Fruit Punch
Dilute two to one with water:
     1 (12 oz.) can frozen grape juice
     concentrate
     1 (12 oz.) can frozen lemonade
     concentrate
     1 (12 oz.) can frozen orange juice
     concentrate
Add before serving:
     1 quart ginger ale
Spoon 1 pint raspberry sherbert over punch
before serving.

Snoopy Punch
     1 (12 oz.) can frozen lemonade concentrate
     1 (12 oz.) can frozen fruit punch concentrate
     1 pint pineapple sherbert
     3 lemons, sliced
     1 quart ginger ale

Add ginger ale just before serving. If you serve this punch to anyone over twelve, you may want to give it a different name. Yields about 40 servings.

Punch Alternatives

If you aren't thrilled with any of these punch recipes, try converting your favorite highball into punch form. For example, a Sea Breeze contains:

    1½ oz. vodka

    2 oz. grapefruit juice (approximately)

    2 oz. cranberry juice (approximately)

In punch form, this would loosely translate to:

    1 liter vodka

    2 quarts grapefruit juice

    2 quarts cranberry juice.

This recipe would make a beautiful, delicious, cool summer punch. Adapt the ingredients to suit your tastes—add more mixer or more vodka to vary the alcohol content.

CHAPTER 4

The Cocktail Party

Cocktail PARTIES ARE like relationships—they can be extremely satisfying, an utter nightmare, or somewhere in between. Unlike relationships, however, the right combination of people isn't always enough to guarantee a good cocktail party. While it's true that a roomful of rotten human beings will usually make for a bad time in any situation, even a party full of your closest friends could turn sour if you fail to plan properly.

Good cocktail party planning involves four steps: buying the right supplies, setting it up, keeping the bar supplied as the party progresses, and knowing when and how to throw everyone out. If you follow each step properly, things should go smoothly. At the very least, if you've planned a good party, you can feel free to blame anything that goes wrong on bad luck. Or bad guests.

Guests are actually the single most important factor in planning and running a party. At almost every step, what you need to do varies according to the kind of party you're having—and the kind of guests you're inviting. For example, if you're having thirty nuns over for drinks, you'll want to buy very different supplies than if you invited the same number of marines. By the same token, if you're planning a twenty-keg fraternity party, you'll want to set up the bar (or bars) differently than you would for Uncle Phil's retirement party. (Obviously, this depends on what kind of person your Uncle Phil is. But you get the point.) Just keep in mind that you're trying to maximize your guests' enjoyment, and adjust accordingly when necessary.

Step 1: Getting the Right Supplies

This is probably the most important step in putting together a successful party. Your guests will forgive you if you put the vodka in the wrong place on the bar or forget to refill the peanut dish, but if you run out of liquor forty-five minutes into a three-hour party, you're not going to make anyone very happy. Although the exact items you may need vary considerably depending on the party, there are certain basic items—liquor, beer, mixers, ice, etc.—that you will need to have on hand for any occasion. Once again, keep your guests in mind as you decide what you'll need.

First, you have to decide what kinds of drinks you would like to serve. The basic cocktail bar includes the following:

- At least two kinds of light alcohol: gin and vodka (usually rum as well and sometimes tequila)
- At least two kinds of dark alcohol: Scotch and bourbon (usually also blended whiskey)
- Two vermouths: dry and sweet
- Wine: white and red (possibly also rosé and fortified wines like port or sherry)
- Beer
- A selection of nonalcoholic drinks

Five variables will influence your liquor selection decisions:

Season: In warm weather, people tend to order light alcohols, beer, and white wine. Conversely, in winter, stock up on dark alcohols, coffee drinks (such as Irish coffee and Mexican coffee), sherry, brandy, and red wine.

Age: Younger people usually prefer light alcohol, blended drinks, wine, beer, and sweet-tasting liqueur cocktails. Older guests drink more dark alcohols, usually unmixed. Buy the highest quality, most prestigious brands you can afford for older, whiskey-drinking guests. They will expect and recognize better names.

Holidays, Themes, and Special Occasions: If the party theme or a holiday season lends itself to special drinks, alter your bar's offerings accordingly. Serve eggnog, hot mulled wine, or punch at a Christmas party; champagne on New Year's Eve; mint juleps on Kentucky Derby Day; green-colored beer on St. Patrick's Day; a red or pink "love potion" punch on Valentine's Day. If your boss is indicted for embezzling funds and has to flee to Mexico, serve margaritas at his going-away party. He probably won't be able to attend, but would no doubt appreciate the gesture.

Time of day: At a ten A.M. brunch bar, don't expect to be making many Zombies, or even gin and tonics. Instead, concentrate on mimosas, screwdrivers, and Bloody Marys. Before dinner, serve light apéritifs—drinks to stimulate appetites, not anesthetize them: for instance, wine, light cocktails, Dubonnet, and kir. As a general rule, add more liquor and more variety as the day progresses, culminating with a fully stocked bar for the eight P.M. to two A.M. crowd.

Guests' preferences: Use your own judgment for other bar adjustments. If your best friend drinks only Sombreros, keep a bottle of Kahlúa at the bar. Consider also that trends these days lean toward an overall preference for light alcohol and sweet drinks.

Liquor

For a typical four-hour cocktail party, buy one 1-liter bottle of liquor for every six guests. Feel free to adjust according to the drinking habits of your guests. Make sure you buy the 1-liter size because it's easier to handle; larger bottles may cost less per drink, but they are bulky, heavy, and often won't take speedpourers. Also, unless you're giving an informal party at home, think twice about buying large bottles and pouring the liquor into smaller containers: this "marrying" of bottles is illegal in many states. You will need only one bottle of each vermouth.

Give a reasonable amount of thought to brand-name selection. Two factors should govern which brands you buy: your budget and your desire to impress the guests. If you're financially secure and you're coordinating a party for the boss—or your future in-laws—buy top-shelf liquor (the name brands considered the highest quality, and usually the most expensive). On a more limited budget for a party with the neighbors—or your current in-laws—you can get by with middle-shelf brands (good quality, recognizable brands, but usually cheaper than top shelf). For a fraternity party, buy bottom-shelf or generic liquor—remember that most college students have very few qualms about drinking "Vodka City" vodka. If you're making punch, you can usually get away with using cheaper brands as long as you mix the punch well out of sight of your guests.

If you must economize, buy cheaper brands of light alcohols; they usually go into mixed drinks, so guests can't taste subtle brand differences. Cutting corners here will allow you to spend more on the higher quality dark alcohols, which people often drink unmixed. For a more extensive discussion of liquor quality and brand selection, see Chapter 5.

To economize without sacrificing name-brand prestige, consider mixing weaker drinks. Make a 1¼-ounce or a 1-ounce highball and the liquor bottles won't empty as quickly. Be careful, however—this may make your harder-drinking guests irate.

When you order for a large party, ask in advance at your local liquor store if you can buy on consignment, which means you can return any unopened, sealed bottles for a refund after the party. Some stores charge extra for this service, but in some situations it's worth the cost.

Beer

For a standard, four-hour cocktail party plan on about one case of beer (24 beers) for every ten guests. Keep in mind that younger crowds tend to drink much more beer than older ones, and the quality of different beers differs even more widely than that of liquors. If you're having 35 guests or more, consider purchasing a quarter keg (about 7.8 gallons—the equivalent of almost 3½ cases, or 83 12-ounce servings). For 70 guests, buy a keg (technically a half keg, which contains 15½ gallons—about 7 cases, or 165 12-ounce servings). Keg beer is economical in the long run, but you will have to leave a deposit on the keg and tap. For the best-tasting beer, move the keg to its party location well ahead of time and keep it consistently cold until empty. Put it in a big tub or barrel, pack chunks of ice around it (try for block ice, which won't melt as fast as cubed or cocktail ice), and cover it with a big plastic bag or towel.

Most kegs use a standard pressure-tap. Take hold of the two small outcropping handles attached to the ring at the base and turn counterclockwise. Then place the tap on the outlet and turn the ring clockwise to screw it into the keg. If you did not turn the ring far enough in the counterclockwise direction, you may find yourself soaked in beer. You can raise the pressure on the stream of beer flowing out by pumping the tap; you can lower the pressure by pulling on the small release pin at the base of the tap. The first few beers coming out of the keg will usually be very foamy. You will have to pump the tap periodically to keep a steady stream flowing as the level of beer in the keg decreases. A very small minority of taps work differently from this one; don't hesitate to ask for more information at the liquor store when you pick up the keg.

Wine

The amount and kind of wine you'll need varies from party to party. A heavy wine-drinking group may consume three or more glasses per person, whereas an older crowd gathered during cold weather would drink only half a glass per person. One case (12 bottles) of wine contains about 60 servings. Generally speaking, younger crowds drink more than older crowds. White wine is more popular in warmer weather, whereas fortified wines, reds, brandies, and sherry are more appropriate in the winter. It would take an entire book to

describe the endless varieties of wines available; ask for help at your liquor store or look for a slightly dry, inexpensive white wine.

Wine comes in bottles containing 750 milliliters, 1½ and 3 liters, and occasionally even larger bottles. Buy whatever size costs the least. It is perfectly appropriate to transfer wine from large bottles to carafes for serving ease and attractiveness.

Punches

For any gathering of fifteen people or more, it might be easier to serve punch in addition to or even instead of other drinks. Punches are especially appropriate for the holiday season, and serving a punch will cut down considerably on the amount of time spent in mixing drinks. Moreover, a good punch recipe will amaze and impress your friends with very little effort on your part. (See the punch recipes in Chapter 3.) The amount you need to make depends on the strength of the punch; count on about four or five servings per person.

Mixers

For every liter of light liquor that you have, you'll need about 2 quarts of mixers. The most common light-alcohol mixers are tonic water, fruit juice, and cola. Whiskey drinkers tend to add less to their liquor, so you can get away with buying less of dark-alcohol mixers, such as soda water, ginger ale, and light soft drinks (1–1½ quarts per liter). Estimate how much of each mixer you'll need and then buy a few extra liters of fruit juice and soft drinks in order to accommodate nondrinking guests. Also, make sure you have diet soda on hand if you're expecting weight-conscious guests.

Ice

Believe it or not, ice is probably the most important of all cocktail ingredients. If you run out of blended whiskey or gin, guests can at least switch to something else. There are no substitutes for ice, however, and just about anyone who's ever had a rum and Coke at room temperature will tell you it's unpleasant. For a typical four-hour party, plan on 1 pound of ice per person. In winter, you could get away with only ¾ pound, and in summer you should buy 1½ pounds per guest. If you want to fill an ice chest for beer and wine, remember to get enough to fill the chest in addition to cocktail ice needs.

Check the Yellow Pages or ask at your liquor store; you may be able to find a local company where you can order ice in quantity (by the 40-pound bag, for example). Some places will deliver right to your home on the day of the party. Make sure to specify cocktail ice when you order so you don't end up taking an ice pick to a 40-pound block.

Garnishes

For a basic bar, limes and lemons are essential, and orange slices are purely optional. Buy one lime for every 4 to 6 guests and cut the limes into wedges in advance. Cuts lemons into twists and slices and cut oranges into slices; you'll need a lemon for every 50 people and an orange for every 25 people. Consider buying a jar each of olives (a must for martinis), cocktail onions (optional—only if you're inviting a Gibson drinker), and cherries (for Manhattans). Fruit-cutting instructions and additional suggestions are in Chapter 1.

Food

You shouldn't consider having a cocktail party of any size without offering some sort of food along with the drinks. At the very least, buy some peanuts, chips, or other snacks. Appetizers—cold vegetables and dip, cheese and crackers, or even more complicated hors d'oeuvres—are better. For more information, buy a cookbook.

Utensils

The basic bartending kit described in Chapter 1 should take care of your utensil needs. Also make sure you have at least one trash barrel, a large ice bucket, a sharp knife for cutting fruit, a water pitcher, a towel, and an ashtray for the bar. An ashtray may seem like a minor detail at this point, but if a line forms at the bar, any smokers in the group will invariably end up flicking burning embers wherever they feel like it.

Napkins

Remember to put out some cocktail napkins for your guests. For a nice touch, place the stack of napkins on the bar, put a shot glass in the center and bear down firmly as you twist the glass clockwise. Remove the glass and you've created a pretty fanned design of cocktail napkins.

Glassware

Real glassware adds a touch of class to any party; on the other hand, glass has a tendency to break. You may want to opt for disposable plastic glasses, which are perfectly acceptable for even relatively highbrow gatherings. You need only two types:

the lowball or on-the-rocks, which is short and wide and holds about 9 ounces, and the highball, which is taller and holds 10 to 12 ounces. Use the highball for popular highballs, beers, and Collinses, and the lowball for everything else—stirred cocktails, shaken drinks, on-the-rocks liquor, and wine. For a four-hour party buy at least two per person, at a ratio of 75 percent highball to 25 percent lowball. For a dance party, plan on at least three per person; people tend to put the glasses down to dance and then forget about them.

If you insist on real glasses, check the phone book for a general rental agency. Some will even deliver the glasses to your home and pick them up again after the party.

Step 2: Setting Up

Once you've gathered all your supplies together, you'll need to set them up in as efficient and attractive a manner as possible. The bar itself can be nothing more complicated than a table that's strong enough to support the weight of all the bottles and the occasional sideways lurch by a tipsy guest. Cover it with a plastic tablecloth for protection from spills, and with a linen tablecloth over that if you're aiming for a classy appearance.

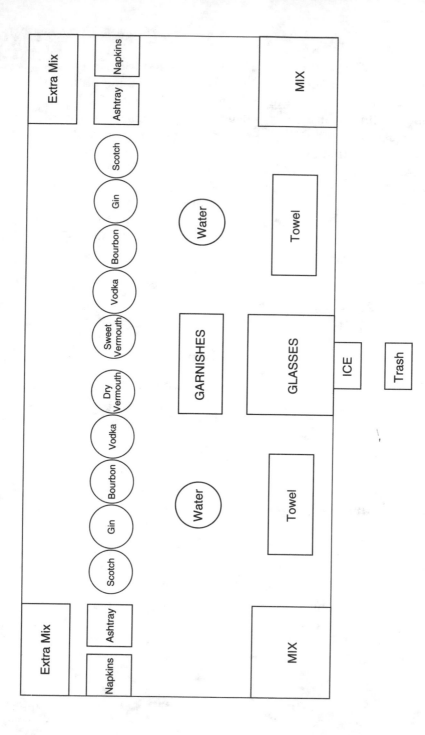

DIAGRAM 1: SELF-SERVICE BAR

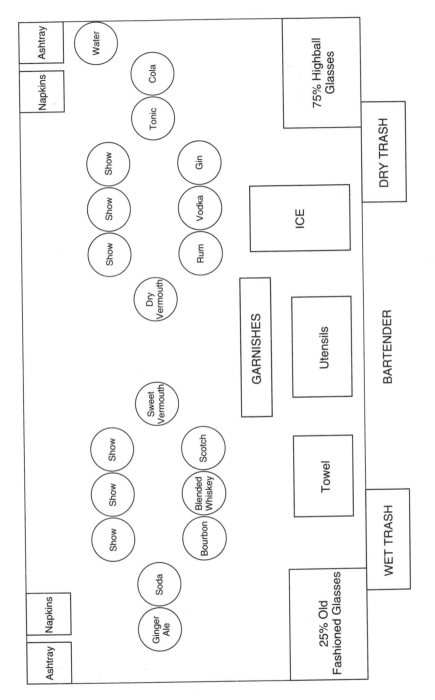

DIAGRAM 2: ONE-PERSON BAR

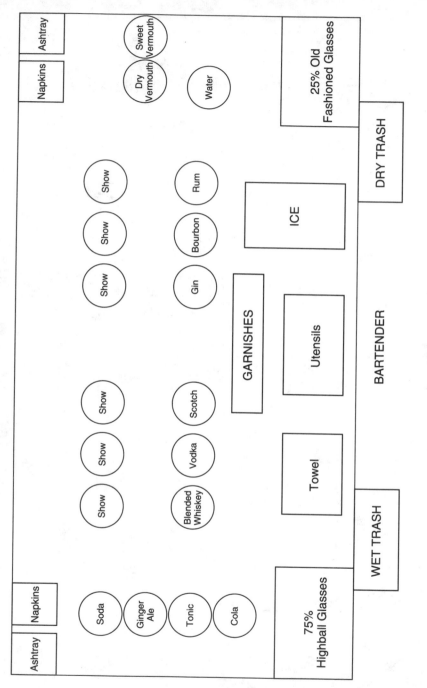

DIAGRAM 3: ONE-PERSON BAR

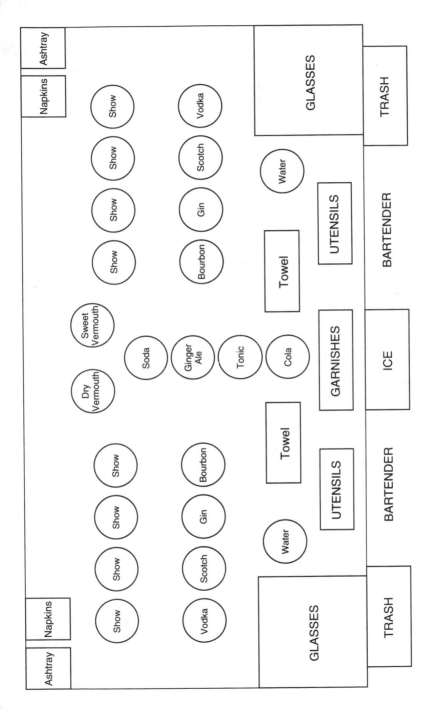

DIAGRAM 4: TWO-PERSON BAR

For small parties (fewer than 15 people), you don't need a bartender. A self-service bar, set up like the one in diagram 1, provides room for two guests to mix their own drinks. Parties of 20 to 100 people tend to run more smoothly with the help of a bartender. Diagrams 2 and 3 illustrate two possible setups for a one-person bar.

Large parties of over 100 guests require the services of at least two bartenders. In diagram 4, notice that the two bartenders share the mixers but have their own liquor bottles for speed and efficiency's sake.

Are you already tired of all this planning? Can't afford a big bash? Have a BYOB party instead—bring your own bottle. At a BYOB, each guest brings a contribution to the bar. It's impossible to diagram a BYOB setup, so you'll just have to improvise.

Use common sense in setting up the party room. Avoid locating it near a doorway, where it will invariably block traffic. Try to put the bar against a wall; if you're tending bar yourself, set it up so that guests can't sneak around you and pour their own drinks. If this happens, your carefully planned, efficient layout will deteriorate rapidly, and in no time your bar will be a mess.

Step 3: Working the Party

Once the party actually starts, all you have to do is ensure that things keep running smoothly at the bar. Once again, how easy this is to accomplish depends on the type of party you're having. To keep things running smoothly, you need to pay attention to two things—keeping the bar orderly and keeping it supplied.

Unless guests are mixing their own drinks, keeping the bar orderly should be simple—just put all of the bottles and utensils back in their original place after you use them, and you shouldn't have to do much more than pick up the occasional empty glass or wadded-up napkin. Take advantage of lulls in the action—whenever the bar clears out for a minute, take the time to tidy things up.

Keeping things supplied is a little more challenging. You'll invariably need to replace items like ice and mixers that may be as far away as the kitchen. This is complicated by a fundamental rule of bartending—*never leave the bar unattended.* The rule holds true for nearly any gathering; even otherwise respectable, trustworthy adults will occasionally show the restraint of hyperactive three-year-olds when left alone around a fully stocked bar.

So you've run out of ice and you're trapped behind the bar? What do you do? Simply ask a friend, a co-worker, or anyone else who's available and won't mind helping to get another bag of ice. If you're in a situation where you don't know anyone at the party, look around for social misfits—the people who have spent more time hovering around the peanut dish than talking to other guests. Every party usually has at least one, and he or she will probably welcome the opportunity to be useful.

It's a good idea to keep a snack—nothing more complicated than peanuts or pretzels is necessary—somewhere near the bar so that guests who are waiting for drinks will have something to occupy themselves with.

For more details on how to look and act professional behind the bar, read Chapter 7. One professional prerequisite discussed there calls for some clarification here: tips. At a private party, a tip cup on the bar looks extremely tacky. On the other hand, if you work at a rather "impersonal" party, such as a large company gathering or some sort of dance, guests may appreciate the option of bribing you for faster or stronger drinks. In situations like this, ask the person who hired you if you may put a tip cup out. If you use one, put a dollar in at the beginning of the night to give guests a hint.

Step 4: Throwing Everybody Out

This is actually much easier than it sounds. When you're ready to call it a night, simply start putting the bar away. First, pack up extra liquor and mixers and take them to the kitchen. Then take speedpourers out of the remaining bottles, put the caps on, and put those bottles away. Guests will quickly notice the absence of liquor; some will be annoyed, but most will eventually start heading home.

At this point, keep a careful eye out for guests who have had too much to drink. *Never let an intoxicated guest drive home.* This is not only extremely dangerous, but also legally actionable—party hosts can be sued for damages caused by drunken guests. If you find yourself in such a situation, either ask a sober guest to drive them home, or offer to drive them yourself.

Party Checklist

Use this list—as well as the ordering summary that follows—as a guide when planning your party. Don't feel obligated to buy everything listed; as always, tailor your purchases to the needs of your guests.

Equipment

shaker glass
shaker shell
strainer
jigger
speedpourers
bar spoon
ice bucket

corkscrew/bottle
opener/can opener
ashtrays
bar napkins
water pitcher
dry and wet trash
buckets
swizzle sticks/cocktail
straws

Liquor

bourbon

blended whiskey

Scotch

vodka

gin

rum

tequila

beer

wine

dry vermouth

sweet vermouth

other liquors?

Mixers

tonic water

cola

soda water

ginger ale

Sprite or 7-Up

diet soda

sour mix

Bloody Mary mix

mixing juices

light cream

milk

water

Rose's lime juice

Glassware (plastic)

lowball

highball

beer

wine

Garbage/Garnishes

lemon twists and slices

lime wedges

orange slices

olives (pitted and

without pimentos)

specialty garnishes (optional)

maraschino cherries (stems on)

cocktail onions

Condiments

bitters

bar sugar

nutmeg

salt

grenadine

Bloody Mary condiments:

Tabasco sauce

Worcestershire sauce

salt and pepper

horseradish

Ordering
Summary

Liquor:	1 liter per 6 guests
	plus beer and wine
Mixer:	2 quarts per liter light alcohol
	1 quart per liter dark alcohol
	plus a selection for nonalcoholic drinks
Ice:	¾ pound per person—winter
	1 pound per person—moderate weather
	1½ pounds per person—summer
	More as needed to fill wine and beer chest
Garnishes:	1 lime per 6 people (more in summer and for young people)
	1 lemon per 50 people
	1 orange per 25 people (optional)
Glasses:	2 per person (more for dance party)
	75 percent highball
	25 percent lowball
Snacks:	varies widely

Party Checklist

Equipment

shaker glass	jigger	ice bucket
shaker shell	speedpourers	ash trays
strainer	bar spoon	bar napkins
water pitcher	dry/wet trash buckets	swizzle sticks
corkscrew/bottle opener/can opener		cocktail straws

Liquor

bourbon	gin	dry vermouth	wine
blended whiskey	rum	sweet vermouth	vodka
Scotch	tequila	other liquors (?)	beer

Mixers

tonic water	Sprite or 7-Up	light cream
cola	diet soda	milk
soda water	sour mix	water
ginger ale	mixing juices	Rose's lime juice
		Bloody Mary mix

Glassware (plastic)

lowball   highball   beer   wine

Garnishes

lemon twists, slices	stemmed maraschino cherries
lime wedges	cocktail onions/olives
orange slices	specialty garnishes (optional)

Condiments

bitters	Bloody Mary condiments
bar sugar	Tabasco sauce
nutmeg	Worcestershire sauce
grenadine	horseradish
	salt and pepper

Putting It All Together—A Sample Party

Still slightly confused? Let's return to an earlier example so you can see how it's done. You're one of the middle managers at a small accounting firm, and the head of the firm suddenly disappears to Mexico after embezzling several million dollars. Your co-workers elect you—ever the social one—to plan a party simultaneously celebrating (or mourning, depending on your point of view) the departure of the old boss and the welcoming of the new one, who it's rumored has a fondness for good Scotch. You plan the party for a Thursday night in June; about 75 people will be attending ranging in age from twenty-three to sixty-five years old, with the majority in their thirties.

Your list of all the supplies you'll need—food excepted (although we'd recommend nachos and quesadillas)—should look something like this:

Liquor	
Smirnoff vodka	13 bottles (1 liter each)
3 Gordon's gin	(These lights cost less
1 Bacardi rum	than expensive imports,
	but have very well-
	respected names.)
1 Chivas Regal Scotch	(Because the boss likes
	Chivas.)
1 Seagram's VO	
1 Early Times bourbon	
2 Jose Cuervo tequila	(Margaritas will be the
1 triple sec	theme drink.)
1 sweet vermouth	(750 ml.)
1 dry vermouth	(750 ml.)

Beer
1 keg Michelob

(Technically a half keg. Michelob is not as expensive as imports; it's a good domestic beer.)

Wine
2 cases white wine

(Whatever is on sale at the store—don't bother to look for Mexican wine, which doesn't exist.)

Mixers (quart bottles)
7 tonic water
3 cola
3 soda
3 ginger ale
2 diet soda
3 grapefruit juice
3 cranberry juice
5 orange juice
1 Bloody Mary mix
Rose's lime juice

(In hot weather, buy lots of mixers, especially for light liquors.)

Ice
4 40-pound bags cocktail ice
1 large block of ice for keg barrel

(3 for drinks, 1 for wine chest)

Plastic glassware
150 highball glasses
50 lowball glasses

(Get the disposable kind that comes in stacks of about 25 per package.)

Garnishes

30 limes	(1 per 5 people in hot
2 lemons	weather, plus 15 more
jar olives	for margaritas)
jar maraschino cherries	
grenadinesalt	(for tequila sunrises)
salt	(for margaritas)

Equipment

bar kit and extra speedpourers	
knife for cutting fruit	
2 trash barrels	(1 for the keg)
ice chest for wine	
water pitcher	
paper towels	

Other supplies
cocktail straws and napkins

It's as easy as that. Just make sure the new boss has a sense of humor before you decide on the theme. . . .

CHAPTER 5

Alcohol—Past and Present

Even IF YOU'RE aiming to become a professional bartender, it's not absolutely essential to know a great deal about the history and varieties of alcohol. The majority of bar patrons are unlikely to confront you with questions like "Hey, barkeep, how many different varietals does the Sonoma Valley produce?" or "Say, what exactly *is* the chemical composition of this Heineken?" Nonetheless, it's a good idea to have at least a little historical and technical knowledge on the subject. In this chapter, we try to address every relevant subject, starting with the chemical process that creates alcohol and moving on to a short history of alcohol in society, followed by brief explanations of the various kinds of alcoholic beverages.

Chemically Speaking. . .

Liquor contains ethyl alcohol (ethanol), as opposed to methyl (wood) or isopropyl (rubbing) alcohol. Of the three varieties, only ethyl alcohol is safe to drink. Ethanol forms as the product of a chemical reaction known as fermentation, in which yeast enzymes decompose carbohydrates into carbon dioxide (CO_2) and ethanol (C_2H_5OH). These carbohydrates come from either grain (in the case of beer and most spirits) or fruit, especially grapes (in the case of wine and some spirits). The carbon dioxide can be left in the alcohol, as in beer, or allowed to evaporate into the atmosphere.

A Very, Very Brief History of Alcohol

Civilization begins with distillation.
—William Faulkner

Faulkner was technically wrong—distillation didn't really come into vogue until the Middle Ages—but his point was correct; historically, almost all of the world's great civilizations have consumed alcohol in some form. Since its use predates written history, no one knows who invented alcohol. There is some evidence that early agricultural societies enjoyed a very primitive form of alcohol. They chewed and spat out grain, then let the mixture ferment; enzymes in the saliva converted the grain starch into sugar and eventually alcohol. Don't try this at home.

More palatable concoctions were developed by societies as far back as ten thousand years ago; at about that time, wine was first produced from grapes in Asia Minor. By 4000 B.C., the Mesopotamians and some Asian societies had discovered viniculture. By 1000 B.C., the Egyptians, Phoenicians, and Chinese had caught on. The Greeks picked up the art of wine-making from the Egyptians and passed it on to the Romans, who during their imperial reign spread it throughout Europe. Early beer production developed concurrently; in the Egypt of the pharaohs, beer-making was entrusted to the temple priests, inaugurating a long tradition of associating alcohol with religion and mysticism (witness the Christian act of communion). Throughout the world, the type of alcohol produced depended on the available resources. For example, African societies used millet to produce beer and the Japanese fermented rice into sake, while viniculture thrived in the Mediterranean and anywhere else grapes could be grown successfully. The English made mead out of honey, while in other parts of Europe barley was used to cultivate beer.

To the would-be martini drinkers of earlier millennia, fermentation had one drawback—the process did not yield beverages with an alcohol content higher than 12 percent. Distillation, the process of altering a substance through heating, was known to the Greeks and others but was not widely practiced. Then, about a thousand years ago, the Scotch and Irish discovered that by extracting much of the water from beer through distillation they could produce a new, potent form of alcohol. They called it *uisge beatha* or *usquebaugh,* which evolved into today's word for the liquor: whiskey. Throughout the British Isles, there was much rejoicing over this discovery, and hangovers got rapidly worse. Soon, alchemists all over Europe were experimenting with distillation and its products, affectionately known as *aqua vitae,* or "water of life." Early methods of distillation were rather crude, leaving a number of impurities in the liquor they produced. It wasn't until the invention of the patent still in the early nineteenth century that it became possible

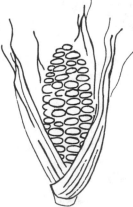

to produce grain neutral spirits, from which most contemporary liquor is made.

Alcohol's position in modern life varies widely from country to country. Its prevalence in ancient civilizations is well documented; the Bible, for example, contains a large number of references to the production and consumption of wine. European societies almost unanimously embrace alcohol consumption as an act of hospitality and sociability; this is also true in Japan. Muslim societies, however, frown upon the use of alcohol—it is prohibited by the Koran, and in most Muslim nations it is illegal. Hindus take a less strongly prohibitive but still negative attitude toward alcohol.

In the United States, alcohol occupies a slightly ambivalent position. During Prohibition (1920–1933), alcohol was illegal according to the 18th Amendment of the Constitution. Prohibition was a disaster—the use of alcohol by the public actually increased during this period, and poorly manufactured "moonshine" greatly increased the health risks associated with drinking. Prohibition is also widely blamed for the ascendance of organized crime, which thrived on the vast black market the new laws created. Today, a variety of mostly Christian fundamentalist religious sects still proscribe the use of alcohol, and a number of "dry" counties in which it is illegal to sell alcohol exist in several Southern states.

Whiskeys

Whiskey, whisky, Scotch, Irish, Canadian, bourbon, rye, blended, straight—whiskeys come in wide and occasionally confusing varieties. Most differ by country of origin, primary base grain, or variations in processing. Some are more or less interchangeable—as a bartender, you should know enough about the different varieties so that you can substitute for them in drinks when necessary.

Whiskey production involves four steps: malting, fermenting, distilling, and aging. That last step imparts color to the whiskey; colorless alcohol goes into wooden barrels to age, and interaction between the wood and the liquor supplies flavor, aroma, and color to the whiskey. As soon as whiskey is bottled, the aging stops.

Whiskey or whisky? Which spelling is correct? If you look at a bottle of Four Roses (American), for example, you will see the word whiskey. Now read one of your Chivas Regal (Scotch) bottles: whisky. As a rule, Scottish and Canadian distillers spell the word without the *e,* and American and Irish whiskey producers include it.

The first qualitative difference is between straight and blended whiskeys. Some blended whiskeys contain mixtures of similar products made by different distillers at different times (as in Scotch); others have combinations of straight whiskeys and neutral, flavorless whiskeys (as in Canadian). Straight whiskeys, on the other hand, are not mixed at all, or are mixed only with whiskey from the same distillation period or distiller.

The country of origin is a second important distinction. Scotch, Irish, Canadian and American whiskeys are all made by different processes and, therefore, have very distinctive tastes.

Scotch, the whisky of Scotland, usually has barley (and sometimes corn) as its primary base grain. Scotch tastes smoky, a flavor it acquires when the barley malt roasts over open peat fires during the first step in production. Then this smoky-flavored malt is combined with water (the mash), fermented, distilled in a pot still, and aged at least three years in uncharred oak barrels or used sherry casks. All Scotches imported to the United States have been aged at least four years; the best ones are twelve years old. Most contain blends of whiskies and have been bottled at 80 to 86 proof.

Irish whiskey, which includes whiskey made in Northern Ireland, uses barley and other grains as its primary bases. Its ingredients and the methods used to make it are similar to those of Scotch. During Irish whiskey production, however, the malt roasts over coal-fired kilns, so Irish whiskey does not have Scotch's smoky flavor. Sometimes the Irish blend their whiskies for a lighter product. It is then aged five to ten years in used sherry casks and bottled at 86 proof.

American whiskeys include bourbon, rye, corn, bottled-in-bond, sour mash, and blended.

Bourbon, named for Bourbon County, Kentucky, where this whiskey originates, is distilled from a fermented mash of at least 51 percent corn. The balance of the mash may contain any other grain, usually rye and barley. The aging process takes two to twelve years in oak barrels, after which the bourbon is bottled at 80 to 90 proof.

Rye whiskey contains at least 51 percent rye grain in its mash. Real rye whiskey (such as Old Overholt) is not as popular as it once was, though, so it usually stays on the back bar. Be alert to this when people order "rye and ginger," for example; they probably want blended whiskey (such as Seagram's 7 or VO). Odd as it may seem, a person who wants to drink real rye usually has to say so rather emphatically: "I want rye—I mean real rye, not that yuppie dishwasher you're serving the kids."

Corn whiskey is distilled from a fermented mash of grain containing at least 80 percent corn. Notice the difference between bourbon (51 percent corn) and corn whiskey (80 percent).

In the United States, bottled-in-bond whiskey is straight whiskey that was bottled at 100 proof and aged at least four years in U.S. government-bonded warehouses.

Sour mashes contain some proportion of previously fermented yeast (as opposed to sweet mash, which is made only from fresh yeast). Jack Daniel's Tennessee Whiskey is made from a sour mash.

The difference between straight and blended American whiskeys may seem confusing at first. Straight means the mash must contain at least 51 percent of a certain grain:

Mash	*Whiskey*
51 percent barley	straight malt whiskey
51 percent rye	straight rye whiskey
51 percent corn	straight bourbon whiskey
80 percent corn	straight corn whiskey

Blended whiskeys are made from combinations of similar straight whiskeys from different distillations or distillers.

Choosing the right whiskey (or whisky) depends on your preferences. At a party, most hosts will provide at least two: Scotch and bourbon (and usually also a blended selection). Professional bars stock a variety of whiskeys, so there you'll have a better chance of finding your favorite type and brand. Every brand whiskey varies in flavor according to its base grains, production techniques, and aging, so it is impossible to generalize about which is best. More expensive brands have probably been made with high quality grains, careful production regulations (for a consistently good whiskey), and longer aging periods. On the other hand, some expensive brands owe their premium price tags in part to having been heavily advertised so that people will pay for their image. Bars, of course, also charge more for these prestige brands.

Gin

Deriving its name from the French *genièvre,* meaning "juniper berry," gin was originally prescribed as a diuretic. Although it has no officially sanctioned medicinal value today, many older people swear that a couple of martinis can cure a wide variety of ailments. Gin is known as "a drinker's drink," meaning a lot of people can't stand the taste of it. Make your own decision.

Gin production involves several steps. First, grains (often corn and rye) are distilled into neutral spirits in a patent still. This grain alcohol is then flavored with juniper berries and other botanicals, distilled again, and bottled at 80 to 100 proof.

Gin brands may vary because of the quality of the raw ingredients, the purity of the added water, and the recipe of flavorings added prior to the second distillation. If you plan to add mixers, subtle brand variations won't matter much, so buy a cheaper brand. After you buy gin, keep the cap on the bottle or it may spoil. After seven to ten days without a cover, gin may taste slightly milky; if it does, throw it away.

Vodka

Historians generally credit Poland with the invention of vodka, perhaps as early as the tenth century A.D. Russians quickly adopted this new spirit and gave it its name: *zhizennia voda,* meaning—like the Latin *aqua vitae*—"water of life." They eventually shortened the word to its affectionate diminutive, *vodka,* which translates literally as "dear little water."

Vodka production involves three basic steps. First, fermented carbohydrates (usually grain) are distilled to at least 190 proof (dear big water) in a patent still. The grain neutral spirits are then diluted, or "cut," with distilled water to 80 to 100 proof, and then filtered through charcoal to remove all distinctive character, aroma, and taste.

This process makes it slightly more difficult to detect variations in quality among vodkas than among other liquors. Nonetheless, brands of vodka still vary because of the quality of the raw materials, the purity of the distilled water added, and the extent of the neutrality achieved by the charcoal filtration. As with gin, if you plan to combine the vodka with mixers, you can probably get away with buying a cheaper brand; the mixer will usually mask the slight imperfections of the cheaper product.

A current trend involves the flavoring of vodka. Vodka may be filtered through foreign juices to produce a distinct flavor, frequently a fruity one. This process is used in the creation of liquors such as Absolut Citron and other flavored vodkas. It should be mentioned that the flavoring process does not noticeably affect the alcohol content of the vodka; although the liquor may taste different, it is still as potent as regular vodka.

Rum

Rum production involves the same basic steps used in making many other liquors: sugarcane juice and molasses (the carbohydrates) are fermented, distilled, sometimes aged, often blended, and then bottled at 80 to 151 proof. Because of variations in this process, you could perhaps find as many kinds of rum as there are brands, but most differ primarily by country of origin.

Puerto Rican rums such as Bacardi, the most common in America, are light-bodied and dry. They are fermented with a special cultured yeast, then distilled in modern patent stills to over 160 proof (fairly neutral), aged at least one year, and blended with other aged rums. Some Puerto Rican rums have an amber or dark color due to aging in charred oak barrels rather than the plain oak casks used for light rum. Virgin Island rums like Ron Virgin taste similar to Puerto Rican rum, but are slightly heavier and usually not aged.

Barbados rum such as Mount Gay also tastes heavier than Puerto Rican rum and has a darker color. Barbados rum is characterized by a soft, rather smoky flavor.

Jamaican rum such as Myers's is the darkest, richest variety. Whereas Puerto Rican production uses a cultured yeast, molasses for Jamaican rum is fermented naturally. Then it is distilled to less than 160 proof (which leaves some of the molasses flavor in the liquor), aged, often colored with caramel to darken the final product, and bottled at 80 to 100 proof.

Rums from other regions, such as Haiti (Rhum Barbancourt), Martinique, and New England (Caldwell's Newburyport) are much less common. All have their own unique characteristics.

Two other Puerto Rican rums merit special recognition. Some specialty drinks (Zombies, for example) call for 151-proof rum as an ingredient. Do not substitute 151-proof rum for regular bar rum (usually around 80 proof); it contains almost twice as much alcohol. On the other hand, spiced Puerto Rican rum, such as Captain Morgan's, can be used as a substitute for regular rums as requested by the drinker. It contains the same amount of alcohol, but with the addition of vanilla and other spices that impart more zest to the drink.

Tequila

Tequila is perhaps the most misunderstood of all liquors. Even some bar books still treat tequila as a mysterious Mexican potion full of worms, hallucinogens, and all manner of vile filth.

Actually, tequila producers must adhere to strict government quality controls, which pretty much take all the mystery—and certainly all the hallucinogens—out of the liquor. Tequila must be made from blue agave plants (*Tequilana weber,* blue variety) grown in a specific, government-designated area of Mexico (which includes the town of Tequila). It must go through two distillations and contain at least 51 percent fermented agave juice.

Production of tequila involves basically the same steps as other distilled spirits: a mixture of at least 51 percent blue agave juice and up to 49 percent sugarcane juice (the carbohydrate) is fermented, distilled twice in pot stills, filtered through charcoal, and then either bottled or aged for one to seven years. Aged tequila, called *anejo,* may be stored in used oak barrels, which gives it a golden color. Tequila is 80 proof in the United States, 96 proof in Mexico.

But what about the worm? You'll find worms only in mescal, not tequila. Mescal is another Mexican liquor, similar to tequila, but it is not subject to the same quality controls; mescal may contain other varieties of the agave from any area of Mexico. The mescal worm is harmless and, despite the innuendos of mescal advertisers, contains no psychoactive elements. Originally, distillers probably put it there because the worm spends its entire life cycle in the agave plant, so burying it in mescal seemed the natural thing to do. Today, the worm in a mescal bottle represents tradition—or merely a sales gimmick.

Brandy

Brandy is distilled from wine or from a fermented fruit mash. If it is made from wine (that is, from grapes), the name brandy stands alone, but if it is distilled from another fruit, brandy is called by the fruit name. For example, apricot brandy contains an apricot base. Some brandies, however, have special names:

Cognac, usually considered the finest of brandies, comes from the Cognac region of France.

Armagnac, another fine brandy, comes from the Gers region of France.

Metaxa is a sweet, dark, grape-based Greek brandy.

Ouzo, another Greek product, is colorless and tastes like licorice.

Calvados, an apple brandy from the Calvados region of France, is similar to applejack, an American apple brandy.

Kirschwasser, or kirsch, is a clear cherry brandy of European origin.

Grappa is a dry, colorless, grape-based Italian Brandy.

Liqueurs

Liqueurs (or cordials) were originally invented as aphrodisiacs; alas, like the worms in a bottle of tequila, this is a lot of nonsense. Today's liqueurs contain various plants, fruits, and other flavorings, and are often very colorful. All contain at least 2.5 percent sugar, but most have much more than that. In fact, the prefix *crème de,* as in crème de menthe and crème de cacao, refers to the high sugar content of the liqueurs, which gives them a creamy consistency.

Liqueurs of the same flavor base generally stand together on the back bar. To help you learn which ones taste similar, and can therefore be interchanged when necessary, the following list offers a partial grouping of common liqueurs according to flavor.

Almond: Amaretto, crème de noyaux, and crème d'almond. Amaretto di Saronno is a high-quality, rather expensive amber-colored liqueur, delicious on its own, in mixed drinks, and in coffee. You may substitute other brands to save money in some drinks, but choose carefully because many do not taste the same as the original.

Crème d'almond and crème de noyaux are similar; you can interchange these red liqueurs in mixed drinks if necessary.

Black currant: Crème de cassis (used for kir).

Black raspberry: Chambord.

Caraway: Kümmel, akavit.

Cherry: Maraschino.

Cocoa: Crème de cacao. Crème de cacao comes in both brown and white (clear). Both colors taste the same, but lend very different appearances to the final drink, so be careful choosing which color to mix.

Coconut and rum: Cocoribe, Malibu.

Coffee: Kahlúa, Tia Maria, coffee brandy. You can sometimes interchange these and other similar products in mixed drinks either to save money or when you've run out of something. People often order Kahlúa by name, though; if they don't (in a drink such as a Sombrero), use coffee brandy instead to save money. Tia Maria contains Jamaican rum with coffee flavoring; a customer may accept it instead of Kahlúa in a pinch.

Cranberry: Boggs, Cranberria.

Cream: Bailey's Irish Cream, Myers's Rum Cream, Belle Bonne, Venetian Cream, toasted almond cream, McGuire's Original Cream, and so on. Sweet cream liqueurs contain cream, alcohol, and flavorings. The alcohol preserves the cream so the liqueur can be stored and served at any temperature. In a sense, these liqueurs are premixed cream cocktails, so they usually contain relatively little alcohol.

Hazelnut: Frangelico.

Herbs and spices: Benedictine D.O.M., B and B (brandy and Benedictine), Campari, Chartreuse, Pimm's No. 1, Pisang Ambon, and others. Benedictine and Chartreuse both date from the sixteenth century and contain secret blends of many herbs and spices. Chartreuse comes in both yellow and green (very light colors) and Benedictine is amber-colored. Campari is a bitter, amber Italian liqueur. Pimm's No. 1 contains herbs, spices, and various fruits in its blend. Pisang Ambon is a green, bitter, orange-and-spice-flavored Dutch liqueur.

Licorice and anise: Absinthe, anisette, Galliano, ouzo (actually a brandy), Pernod, sambuca. Absinthe contains a dangerous narcotic ingredient (wormwood) and is illegal in the United States, so use Pernod as a substitute. Galliano, a golden vanilla-licorice liqueur, comes in a very tall bottle and goes into drinks containing the word Golden, such as Golden Dream and Golden Cadillac.

Melon: Midori. Many other melon liqueurs have appeared on the market in the wake of Midori's success. Taste them before trying to substitute to make sure they taste the same as Midori; many aren't as good, but some will blend nicely into mixed drinks.

Mint: Crème de menthe, peppermint schnapps. Crème de menthe comes in two colors: green and white (clear). Many people drink it as an after-dinner cordial, or between courses of a meal to clean the palate. Consider color in deciding which crème de menthe to put into a mixed drink. Most recipes will tell you which one to use.

Schnapps: A clear, light-bodied crème de menthe, schnapps is popular on the rocks, as a shot, and in some mixed drinks.

Orange: Grand Marnier, Cointreau, triple sec, curaçao. Cointreau (clear, bittersweet) and Grand Marnier (orange-colored, cognac-based) are brand-name orange liqueurs. Curaçao comes in both orange and a pretty blue. Make sure you use orange when no color is specified, and blue when the recipe says blue curaçao. Triple sec, a clear, tart liqueur, is not as sweet as curaçao. When a recipe calls for Cointreau and you don't have it or you're trying to save money, substitute triple sec.

Sloe berry: Sloe gin. Sloe gin, neither slow nor gin, obtains its flavor from sloe berries, the fruit of the blackthorn bush. This red liqueur is popular in sloe gin fizzes and Sloe Screws.

Violet: Crème de violette, Crème Yvette, Parfait Amour. These liqueurs are violet-flavored and -colored.

Whiskey: Drambuie, Irish Mist, Southern Comfort, Rock

and Rye, and others. Whiskey and honey combine in two popular liqueurs: Drambuie, which is Scotch-based, and Irish Mist, made of Irish whiskey. Southern Comfort is a bourbon-based, sweet-tasting, 100-proof liqueur flavored with peaches and other ingredients. Drinks with the word Comfortable or Comfort in their names contain Southern Comfort. Rock and Rye is rye whiskey flavored with fruit and rock candy.

    Yogurt and Cognac: Trenais.

The list is admittedly incomplete. New liqueurs are being introduced even as you read these words, and a good bartender must stay on top of current trends and new products. You should not be afraid to talk to suppliers to get ideas of new trends or what's new in the bartending field. However, don't forget your most valuable gauge of new trends, the customer. Pay attention to what drinks your customers are ordering and take time to learn the latest recipes.

Liquor Quality Classification

Even if you're not much of a drinker, you probably have some concept of brand classification. You might have heard one friend *ooh* and *aah* over a gift of Glenfiddich, or another refuse to drink anything but Tanqueray. Maybe you've noticed that some advertisements have a certain air about them—one of class and prestige, usually conveyed by photographs of rich people playing billiards. On the other end of the spectrum, perhaps, you may have personally experienced the effect that a three-dollar bottle of wine can have on the digestive system.

    The accepted way to designate liquor quality in bartending is by the "shelf." High-quality, prestige brands are "top shelf"; good, less expensive brands are "middle shelf"; and cheaper brands or generic liquors are classified as "bottom shelf" or "speed-rack."

    In most bars, customers pay more for "call" brands—

those top- and middle-shelf brands that they ask for by name. Managers have devised various systems to let the bartender know how much to charge: a colored dot on the bottle, a list by the cash register, or just a general rule that certain shelves on the bar cost more.

For your home bar, buy the brands you like best. If you're completely at a loss, don't hesitate to ask friends or a local liquor store clerk for advice.

Beer

While wine aficionados may argue the point, beer is probably the oldest of all alcoholic beverages. Over the years, the world has accumulated a lot of different brands of beer; however, all beers are brewed in much the same way that they have been since before the time of Christ. The following steps describe a basic brewing process:

1. Malt preparation: The brewer steeps barley (other carbohydrates may be used, but barley is most common) in water and heats it to begin the beer-making process. This step imparts color and taste to the beer; depending on the degree of roasting, the final product will be either pale and light or dark and robust.

2. Mashing: Mashing involves a rather complicated process for preparing the malted barley. The malt enzymes break down the starch to sugar and the complex protein of the malt to simpler nitrogen compounds.

3. Lautering: The brewer removes spent grains and continues brewing the liquid.

4. Boiling and hopping: The liquid is poured into huge kettles and boiled for about two hours, during which time hops are added to the brew. Hops, the dried flower cones of the hop vine, give beer a sharp, bitter flavor, which is a nice balance to the sweetness of malt sugars. Hops also contribute a pleasant aroma to the brew and help preserve freshness. This unfermented mixture of malted barley and hops is called the wort.

5. Hops separation and cooling: After the wort has taken on the flavor of the hops, they are removed and the brew passes through a cooling device.

6. Fermentation: The wort is transferred to fermenting vessels, and yeast is added. The yeast, which consists of living, single-celled fungi, takes the sugar in the brew and breaks it down into carbon dioxide and alcohol. The brewer can use two species of yeast and, depending on which he chooses, produce ale or lager.

7. Storage: After fermentation, the beer is cooled and placed in storage for at least two to four weeks.

8. Packaging: The beer is bottled and passes through a pasteurizer where the temperature of the beer is raised to 140°F. to kill the yeast, then cooled to room temperature. The bottles are then capped and sold.

The word "beer" generally covers both ale and lager, although many people use it specifically as a synonym for lager. Both products undergo basically the same brewing process, but a few variations account for the distinctly different tastes of the two.

Lager is brewed at relatively low temperatures (around 131°F.) using a "bottom-fermenting" yeast, meaning a yeast that works mostly from the bottom of the barrel. The brewer then draws the lager off the top, leaving the yeast in the tank. Most popular, mass-produced American beers are lagers. By contrast, ale is brewed at higher temperatures (around 140°F.) using a "top-fermenting" yeast—a yeast that floats on the top of the brew during fermentation and then must be skimmed off. Ale tastes hoppier (more bitter) than lager and has a higher alcohol content (4.4 to 5.5 percent, opposed to lager's

3.2 to 4.5 percent). Popular ales include Molson Golden, Ballantine, and Bass.

Pilsner beer (such as Pilsner Urquell) is a kind of lager beer named for the famous brews of Pilsen, Czechoslovakia. As a bartender, you will serve a lot of "light" Pilsners (Miller Lite, Amstel Light), which were brewed with extra enzymes and therefore have lower calorie, carbohydrate, and alcohol contents. Light beers contain 68 to 134 calories per 12 ounces (other beers have 150 to 180 calories) and 2.5 to 3.2 percent alcohol.

Porter and stout are sweet, dark, brown ales. Stout (such as Guinness) tastes slightly hoppier than porter (Narrangansett, Anchor), has a thicker texture, and contains 5 to 6 percent alcohol.

Malt liquor (Colt 45, King Cobra) is a lager that has a higher alcohol content than other lagers (over 5 percent). It tastes hoppier than beer, yet lighter than ale.

Bock beer (such as Genesee Bock) is a sweet, heavy, amber-to-dark-colored lager beer containing 3.5 percent alcohol.

To help you keep track of all these different beers, here's a quick summary:

Lagers	*Ales*
Light-colored lager	Pale Ale
Dark lager	Brown Ale
Pilsner	Porter
Light beer	Stout
Malt liquor	
Bock	

Unlike many wines and a few people, beer does not get better with age—in fact, beer does not keep well at all. Bottled beer has a peak life expectancy of only six months, canned beer half that time, and kegs (which are unpasteurized) only one month. Keep this in mind when you see amazing beer sales—any time you see a beer priced considerably lower than it usually is, it's a safe bet that it's getting old. This does not mean that it's not drinkable; however, you should resist the urge to stock up on huge quantities of beer that will probably start to turn on you in a couple of weeks.

Beer is sensitive to temperature extremes and to light, so store it in a cool, dark area—your refrigerator, for example. The ideal temperature is somewhere between 40 and 60 degrees Fahrenheit. At higher temperatures, the ingredients break down and the aroma and flavor deteriorate, resulting in "skunked" beer. When frozen, the solids separate from the liquid and form flakes that do not go back into solution when the beer thaws.

Keg beer (also called "draft or "tap") demands extra-special attention. It is not pasteurized and must be refrigerated at all times. (For more information about kegs, see pages 22 and 132–33.)

Several brewers have come out with "beer balls" as a smaller alternative to the keg. These 5⅙-gallon, spherical, plastic minikegs may be more convenient than bottles or cans in states with returnable bottle laws. They also look extremely silly.

To serve the perfect beer, start with a sparkling clean beer glass dipped in cold water. You should keep special glasses just for beer; a film on the glass—from milk or detergent, for example—can alter the taste of the beer. For a thick, foamy head, pour the beer straight down the middle of the glass from about one inch above the rim. For a smaller head, tilt the glass and pour down the side; then, before it is completely filled bring it upright.

Wine

Not only does one drink wine, but one inhales it, one looks at it, one tastes it, one swallows it . . . and then one talks about it.

—King Edward VII

The first thing you should know about wine is this: like King Edward, a lot of connoisseurs are extremely pompous, snooty people. If you find yourself in a conversation with one of these people and can't immediately name the three best years for Bordeaux wines in the last century, you may very well be sniffed at mercilessly.

Do not, however, let this deter you. Despite what the experts would like you to believe, you do not need to know a lot about wine to enjoy it. Serious wine appreciation can involve a staggering amount of detail; however, a few basics— the different types of grapes and the different wine-growing regions, for example—are all you'll need to know to purchase and enjoy wine intelligently.

As you begin to experiment with different wines, remember which wines you like best. Wine appreciation is subjective, and when you know what you like, you'll be able to choose accordingly in almost any situation. Prices are not always the best indicators of quality—it's entirely possible to find a seven-dollar bottle of wine that you like just as much as a seventy-dollar one. To find a good wine at a reasonable price, look for sales and if you have any questions, don't hesitate to ask the wine store clerk for advice.

Wines are classified as still, sparkling, or fortified. Still wines are noncarbonated beverages containing 7 to 15 percent alcohol. The three basic kinds of still wine are red, white, and rosé. Sparkling wines, such as champagne, sparkling burgundy, and Asti Spumante, may also be red, white, or rosé, with 7 to 15 percent alcohol, but they are all bubbly. Fortified wines, such as port and sherry, contain brandy, which brings the alcohol content up to 18 to 22 percent. Dubonnet and vermouth have other flavorings added as well as brandy and are called "aromatics."

Most common wines are still. Interestingly enough, their red, white, or rose color does *not* indicate what color grapes the wine came from, but instead the length of time the grape skins stayed in the wine during fermentation.

Aside from color, wines are classified according to their place of origin, grape variety, and vintage year. All of this information is contained on the wine label—if it's not, you're probably dealing with a very cheap wine. Vintage is less important to novice wine drinkers than the place of origin and the grape variety.

Wine is made all over the world in an ever increasing number of countries. Some of the largest wine-producing countries are the United States, France, Germany, Italy, Portugal, Spain, Chile, Australia, and Japan. Japanese wine, called sake, is made from rice instead of grapes. Within most of these countries are a large variety of wine-producing regions, and wines frequently take their name from the region in which they're produced. For example, chablis is a white wine from the Chablis region in France, while burgundy is a red wine from the Burgundy region. Wine makers will occasionally take liberties with these designations—many American wines are known as chablis despite the fact that they are produced in the United States.

Many wines, including all of those produced in California, are referred to by the names of varieties of grapes, provided that the wine contains at least 51 percent of a certain grape. Some common "varietal" white wines include, from driest to sweetest, chardonnay, fumé blanc, chenin blanc, riesling, and sauterne. White zinfandel is a sweet white wine made from red zinfandel grapes, which lends it a pinkish color. Common red varietals include zinfandel, pinot noir, merlot, and cabernet sauvignon.

In the United States, white wine outsells red and rosé by about 5 to 1. If you're stocking a bar on a limited budget, buy white. Dry to medium white wines meet with more universal approval than sweet wines, which make some drinkers queasy.

In storage, keep wine bottles on their sides so the corks will stay moist, and protect them from temperature extremes and light. As a general rule, serve red wine at room temperature and white wine chilled. If you're serving wine with food, tradition dictates that red wines go well with beef, pork, and lamb, while white wines are better suited to poultry and fish.

CHAPTER 6

Side Effects

Like JUST ABOUT everything, alcohol is best enjoyed in moderation. A glass or two of wine with dinner, hot buttered rum by the fireplace on a cold winter day, a hot dog and a beer at the ball park—scenes like these are so idyllic, they make alcohol advertisements seem almost believable. Taken at the right time and in reasonable amounts, alcohol can genuinely enhance your life.

Unfortunately, alcohol can ruin your life as well. Some of the damage that alcohol wreaks on the careless and stupid is minor enough to be almost amusing. Remember the worst hangover of your life? Most people do, in vivid and graphic detail. The average college student, for example, knows more synonyms for vomiting than the average Eskimo does for snow. A "beer gut" can also be good for a laugh, especially when it belongs to someone else.

Other alcohol-related problems, however, are less easy to joke about. An overdose of alcohol can be fatal even to the healthiest person. Alcoholism—once considered the province of bums and winos—is now universally recognized as a disease that can strike people from any social or economic group.

Finally, drunk drivers account for nearly half of all American traffic fatalities, and many of the victims of these accidents are innocent motorists who just happened to be on the wrong road at the wrong time.

Alcohol is a drug—it can be both used and abused. Whether you plan to serve it or just drink it, you should be aware of its side effects. In this chapter, we'll discuss:

The physiology of alcohol: How the body metabolizes alcohol. How a person becomes drunk. How much an individual can drink before being considered drunk.

Hangovers: The causes of hangovers. Modern science's unsuccessful quest for a cure.

Other side effects: Liquor's effect on other parts of the body besides the brain. The direct link between alcohol and unsightly weight problems.

Serious side effects: Alcohol abuse and the problem drinker. Drinking and driving.

Bartenders' and hosts' responsibilities: Legal issues.

Physiology: The Brain Drain

Your body actually produces small amounts of alcohol naturally, transforming food sugars into about one ounce of ethanol each day. When it takes in additional alcohol, however, the excess is absorbed into the bloodstream and affects various parts of the body until the alcohol eventually oxidizes.

Liquor contains ethyl alcohol. The primary distinction between ethyl and other alcohols is that ethanol metabolizes rapidly into relatively harmless substances, whereas the other alcohols metabolize slowly into poisons. It is extremely unwise to drink any type of alcohol other than ethyl. Even a small amount of isopropyl (rubbing) alcohol can cause permanent blindness, and a larger amount can be fatal.

Three basic steps take place when the body processes alcohol: absorption, distribution, and oxidation. In the absorption phase, alcohol—unlike most foods—passes rapidly into the bloodstream without being digested. Certain variables alter this process. Have you ever noticed that you get drunk faster on an empty stomach? Food keeps alcohol in the stomach longer (where absorption takes place rapidly). Bear in mind, however, that the alcohol will eventually make it to the small intestine, so gorging yourself will only delay the effects. Does champagne make you feel tipsy faster than wine? Bubbles make you get drunker faster. The carbon dioxide in any carbonated drink hastens the movement of alcohol through the stomach to the small intestine and into the bloodstream.

Body weight is also a major consideration in the attempt to gauge alcohol's effect on the drinker. Since the bloodstream distributes alcohol uniformly throughout the body, larger people—whose bloodstreams cover a lot more ground—will feel the effect of a given number of drinks less strongly than smaller people.

Once the alcohol enters the bloodstream, it passes to body organs in proportion to the amount of water they contain. The most immediate and noticeable characteristics of drunkenness occur as a result of alcohol's effect on the brain, which contains a high concentration of water. The most pronounced brain responses vary directly with the amount of alcohol measured in the bloodstream. For that reason, a fairly good indication of intoxication is a measurement called the blood alcohol concentration (BAC), the percentage of alcohol in the bloodstream. (Sometimes this measurement is referred to as the BAL, blood alcohol level.) Alcohol is a depressant, so when the BAC rises, more areas of the brain become depressed.

Reactions to alcohol vary tremendously among individuals, but when the BAC reaches .05 percent in the average person, the outer layer of the brain becomes drugged and sluggish. This outer layer controls inhibitions, self-restraint, and judgment—or, rather, it did when it was sober. When alcohol numbs this control center, most inhibitions fly out the window, and drinkers usually find they have a lot more to say about everything. Given this newfound sociability and vivaciousness, people often forget that alcohol is a depressant. After all, any drug that leads you to call your boss a clown to his face *must* be a stimulant. Remember, however, that this feeling stems from the depression of a brain part, not the stimulation of it.

At a BAC of .10 percent, the motor area of the brain (anterior) becomes depressed and coordination becomes quite impaired. The drinker staggers, slurs words, and can't quite fit the key in the keyhole. By this point, just about all inhibitions have been drowned.

At .20 percent BAC, alcohol affects the midbrain, the section that controls emotional behavior. At this stage, it is next to impossible for the drinker to appear sober. Sensory and motor skills have deteriorated to the point where many drinkers need to lie down. Some laugh, some cry, some become angry, some feel romantic . . . and some feel all these emotions at the same time.

A .30 percent BAC depresses the lower portion of the brain, which controls sensory perception. At this level, drinkers virtually lose consciousness; although awake, they have very little comprehension of the world around them. As the saying goes, "The lights are on, but nobody's home." This is the point at which many drinkers "black out"—after sobering up, they will have no memory of their actions. Considering the way most people with a .30 percent act, this can be a blessing.

Between .35 and .45 percent BAC, the party's over. A drinker at this level enters a coma and should be brought to a hospital. A BAC of .35 percent is generally the minimum level which causes death, so a coma is the body's defense mechanism against death. In this state, a patient will not drink anymore, so the body stands a better chance of keeping its BAC down to a survivable level.

At .60 percent BAC, the part of the brain that controls

those little everyday activities like breathing and heartbeat becomes depressed. At this point, fatality is usually inevitable. A .60 BAC is actually easier to reach than you might think—chugging a fifth of liquor, for example, will probably kill you in ten minutes.

The following list summarizes the effects of the blood alcohol concentration (BAC) on the brain of an average person. These responses vary, however, from person to person and from day to day—see below for an explanation of other factors that affect intoxication. The second list approximates the number of drinks it takes the average person to reach these levels.

BAC (%)	Effects
.05	Release of inhibitions and self-restraint; poor judgment
.10	Loss of coordination; staggering, slurring clumsiness, impaired vision
.20	Dulled sensory perception; loss of emotional control
.30	Virtual loss of consciousness; blackout
.35–.45	Coma; minimum lethal level
.60	Death

Other Factors Influencing Intoxication

Weight/alcohol consumption data such as shown here provide a handy drinking formula that allows you to figure out how drunk you will be after each drink. Do not rely on these charts. The only variables they take into consideration are weight, time, number of drinks consumed, and sometimes sex (to account for different metabolisms). In reality, many other factors play an important role in determining degrees of intoxication.

Sleep: How much sleep did the drinker get last night? A tired person will show the effects of alcohol more readily than an alert drinker.

Relationships Among Sex, Weight, Oral Alcohol Consumption, and Blood Alcohol Level

Blood Alcohol Levels (mg/100 ml)

Alcohol (oz.)	Drinks* per hr.	Female 100 lbs	Female 150 lbs	Male 150 lbs	Male 200 lbs
½	1	.045	.03	.025	.019
1	2	.09	.06	.05	.037
2	4	.18	.12	.10	.07
3	6	.27	.18	.15	.11
4	8	.36	.24	.20	.15
5	10	.45	.30	.25	.18

*1 ounce of 100-proof spirits, a 12-oz. beer, 5 oz. of wine, or 3 oz. of sherry.
SOURCE: Ray, Oakley: *Drugs, Society and Human Behavior*, 3d ed. (St. Louis: C. V. Mosby Co., 1983). Used by permission.

Other drugs: Did the drinker take any medication? Medicine alters alcohol's effects, sometimes drastically. Be very cautious mixing any two drugs, especially when one of them is alcohol.

Age: Younger people usually become drunk on fewer drinks. Among older drinkers, vision generally deteriorates more rapidly as the BAC increases.

Mood: Is the drinker in a good mood? An especially happy, sad, angry, or other mood probably will alter the person's response to alcohol.

Metabolism: How does the drinker's metabolism work? Some people oxidize alcohol faster than others. As a result, BAC can vary widely even when many other factors remain constant.

Liver function: The organ, not the food . . . A healthy liver plays a major role in the sobering process and thus greatly influences the degree of inebriation.

> One faulty assumption people often make is that beer or wine will not get them as drunk as a drink made with higher-proof liquor. Wrong. A cocktail, a beer, a 5-ounce glass of wine, and a 3-ounce glass of sherry all have about the same amount of pure alcohol in them (.6 ounces).

Sobering Up

Although alcohol moves quickly into the body and takes rapid effect, getting it out of the system takes a long time. Sobering up occurs through a process called oxidation, in which the liver breaks alcohol down into water and carbon dioxide. In the case of most foods, the rate of oxidation increases with activity. That is, as the body needs more energy, it breaks down the food faster. Alcohol, however, has a constant rate of oxidation that cannot be increased through exercise. For most people, that rate is about half an ounce of alcohol (about one drink) per hour.

In other words, sobering up is simply a matter of time. All the black coffee, brisk walks, fresh air, and cold showers in the world will not speed it up.

The Hangover

Headache. Nausea. Stomach pains. An almost indescribable thirst. And—good lord, who's that person on the other side of the bed???

Hangovers can be remarkably debilitating. Drink a pint or two of tequila, and chances are you won't spend more than half of the next day out of bed. Unless, of course, you have to go to work—in which case you'll spend more than the day wishing you were still in bed. While hangovers vary widely depending on a number of factors, too much of any kind of alcohol will inevitably give you one.

Most of the agony you feel when you're hung over is caused by dehydration. Remember the thirteen trips you took to the bathroom during last night's blowout? When the body processes alcohol, it uses up large amounts of water; this will not only make you very thirsty in the morning but will produce a headache and an overall feeling of sluggishness.

The variety of additives and spices added to liquor during production and mixing comprise the second major hangover culprit. Your nausea and stomach pains can be attributed in part to a number of flavoring herbs and spices in the liquor itself; as a general rule, cheaper liquor is more likely to contain impurities and hangover-inducing additives, and liqueurs are more likely than other spirits to contain herbs and spices that will upset your stomach. Certain mixers can also lead to trouble—for example, the citric acid contained in orange juice of an evening's worth of screwdrivers will probably not do your digestive system any favors.

Unfortunately, there is no reliable "cure" for a hangover. Only time—and, if possible, a long afternoon nap—will heal your self-inflicted wounds. There are, however, a few things you can do to minimize the pain.

First, drink plenty of water before bed. Drink until you're full and then drink some more. Keep a pitcher of water beside your bed in case you wake up during the night, so you can drink more. Depending on your level of drunkenness, this should counteract a great deal of the dehydration that causes hangovers. If you fell asleep before drinking water the night before, drink plenty the next morning. Resist the temptation to drink orange juice, because the acid in it might make your stomach pains feel worse.

Second, take a shower, sauna, or steam bath in the morning (not too long in the sauna or steam bath). Any of these will increase circulation and refresh and open pores, which should make you feel refreshed.

Third, take a nonaspirin pain reliever. You should avoid aspirin, which may upset your stomach. A couple of these pain relievers, especially after drinking a lot of water the night before, should reduce headache pain and other general body aches.

Even if you're really drunk and can't face the possibility of a massive hangover, avoid the temptation to empty your stomach. Although vomiting will prevent most of the alcohol left in your stomach from passing into the bloodstream and will rid your stomach of all those irritating additives, spices, and mixers, the harmful physiological side effects of induced vomiting far outweigh even the worst of hangovers. If the body decides to "clean house," you won't need to make yourself sick.

An old English proverb recommends taking "a hair of the dog that bit you" in order to cure a hangover—that is, to take a small amount of alcohol the next day. This will postpone but probably not eliminate your hangover; furthermore, taking a restorative morning drink is a habit that's very likely to lead to alcoholism. As such, it's extremely inadvisable.

Other Side Effects

Fat

If you're weight-conscious, alcohol is the worst of both worlds—it has absolutely no nutritional value, yet it contains a large number of calories. Even worse, the mixers that you usually ingest along with most liquors tend to be very fattening as well. The calorie counts may vary depending on the recipe. But if you're watching your weight and would like a drink, try a light beer, a glass of wine, a wine spritzer or cooler, or perhaps the pineapple-wine cooler listed on page 106. If you prefer a distilled spirit, drink it either without the mixer, with soda water, or with a low-calorie mixer. Take a look at the following charts:

Alcoholic Beverage	Amount	Calories
Beer, ale	12 oz.	about 150
Light beer	12 oz.	about 95
Distilled liquors		
80 proof	1½ oz.	97
86 proof	1½ oz.	105
94 proof	1½ oz.	116
Dry table wine	4 oz.	75–100

Mixers	Amount	Calories
Soda water	any	0
Cola	8 oz.	96
Ginger ale	8 oz.	72
Tonic water	8 oz.	72
Sour mix	4 oz.	about 50
Orange juice	8 oz.	100
Cranberry juice	8 oz.	145

If you think that's bad . . .

Drink	Amount	Calories
Margarita	12 oz.	375
Piña colada	12 oz.	350
Sangría	12 oz.	250
Frozen daiquiri	12 oz.	300
Strawberry daiquiri	12 oz.	350
Tom Collins	12 oz.	225

Other short-term effects

The brain isn't the only part of your body to notice the presence of alcohol. Even just one drink causes some rather harmless changes in the body; more liquor provokes more serious reactions.

The first drink or two affects the digestive system. It stimulates gastric juices in the stomach and possibly provokes a reaction in the taste buds, both of which serve to increase appetite. For this reason, people often enjoy apéritifs before meals. Apéritifs, alcoholic beverages drunk before the meal to stimulate the appetite, should be rather low in alcohol and not too warm or cold. A glass of wine, a beer, or a cocktail fits this description and serves as a good apéritif.

Too much alcohol might have the opposite effect—it will stop digestion and probably deaden taste buds, thus reducing appetite. On the other hand, some people eat every potato chip in sight whenever they drink too much. This is due more properly to the lowering of inhibitions in the brain than to any direct effect on the digestive system—when the inhibitions go, so does the diet.

When alcohol depresses the brain, many of the bodily functions that are regulated by the brain are also impaired. For instance, alcohol throws off the body's water balance, which causes the kidneys to excrete excessive amounts of water. This imbalance explains part of the dehydration problem of hangovers.

An alcohol-drugged brain also results in a lack of motor skills and sensory perception while at the same time promoting a feeling of self-confidence and sociability. This combination of effects presents a number of problems in other areas of the body. As Shakespeare noted in *Macbeth,* "It provokes the desire, but it takes away the performance." Impaired sexual performance is only one ego-deflating response of the body to a sluggish brain.

The side effects of alcohol should pose no serious threat to the moderate drinker. In fact, some studies reveal that small quantities of alcohol may even be good for you; moderate amounts of red wine, for example, have been shown to be effective in helping prevent certain types of heart disease. At any rate, moderate and responsible drinking generally will not lead to health problems.

Alcoholism

Once wrongly considered to be a weakness rather than a disease, alcoholism is still a somewhat mysterious illness. While an estimated 10.5 million people in the United States alone are alcoholics, alcoholism's causes are only partially understood. A variety of factors, both internal and external, have been linked to the development of the disease. The children of alcoholics are more likely than others to contract the disease; on the other hand, plenty of alcoholics have no family history of abuse. Certain personality traits—impulsivity, nonconformity, a sense of alienation—are shared by many alcoholics, yet it is unclear whether these are causes or merely symptoms of the disease. Emotional problems and stress can lead to substance abuse in almost any person; alcoholics frequently use liquor to mask emotional pain or negative feelings. Social acceptability also plays a distinct role. Many college students, for example, exhibit symptoms of alcoholism that disappear once they leave the beer-soaked hallways of undergraduate life.

Whatever its causes, there are a number of symptoms that point to alcoholism:

1. Occasional "binges"—periods of uncontrolled drinking.
2. Drinking in order to get drunk; or an inability to stop at just one or two drinks.
3. An increasing tolerance to alcohol—using larger and larger quantities of alcohol to achieve the same effect.

4. Work- or school-related problems that are caused by drinking; personal problems caused by drinking.
5. Avoiding family or friends when drinking; irritation at any discussion of your drinking by family or friends.
6. Failure to keep promises to yourself about controlling or cutting down your drinking.
7. Feelings of guilt about drinking; frequent regret over things you have said or done when drunk.
8. Frequent blackouts.
9. Irregular eating habits during periods of heavy drinking.
10. Using alcohol as an escape from personal problems.

This is only a partial list, but it covers most of the bases. Number 4 is probably the most obvious symptom of alcoholism.

While its causes are unclear, the effects of alcoholism are well known. Alcohol abuse leads to a myriad of personal and professional problems: alcoholics frequently lose their jobs, friends, spouses, and children because of their inability to avoid regular heavy drinking. Suicide rates are also consistently high among alcoholics.

These emotional problems become compounded by the inevitable destruction of the chronic alcoholic's body. Physically addicted to liquor, chronic alcoholics often suffer delirium tremens (DTs) when withdrawing from alcohol without proper medical care. DTs involve three to six days of shaking, fever, acute panic, and vivid hallucinations. This experience sometimes frightens the problem drinker away from alcohol for a while but, unfortunately, many eventually return to their previous condition.

After years of addiction, many chronic alcoholics virtually stop eating, as alcohol replaces the calories food once provided. Since alcohol has no nutritional value, most alcoholics develop serious vitamin and mineral deficiencies as well as diseases which accompany such malnutrition. Beriberi, a condition resulting from vitamin B shortages, often reveals itself in the alcoholic as Korsakoff's psychosis or Wernicke's syndrome, both characterized by gradual memory loss, confusion, and disorientation.

The liver, which plays such a large role in processing alcohol in the body, takes a tremendous beating. After just two days of heavy drinking, a person can develop fatty liver as the result of a breakdown in the mechanism which moves fat from the liver into the blood. Very long periods of drinking increase the severity of this condition, or may lead to alcoholic hepatitis, and inflammation of the liver. Some alcoholics' livers become scarred and hardened from abuse. This condition, known as cirrhosis, is a leading cause of death in many areas of the country.

Long-term heavy drinking may also lead to destruction within the digestive and circulatory systems. Many alcoholics develop chronic irritation of the stomach lining as the result of alcohol's constant stimulation of gastric fluids. Some contract cancer of the mouth, pharynx, larynx, or esophagus. After a long period of regularly taxing the heart, alcoholism may also give rise to heart diseases and an increased risk of high blood pressure.

Technically, alcoholism is incurable—complete abstinence allows alcoholics to lead normal lives, but most will never be able to enjoy even a social drink. Today, most rehabilitation programs revolve around detoxification. Medical professionals supervise the alcoholic's withdrawal, treat DT symptoms, provide medical care for physical ailments, and offer psychological guidance to ease the reformed alcoholic into a life of abstinence. Support groups such as Alcoholics Anonymous also help an alcoholic stay on the wagon.

Drunk Driving

Simply put, driving drunk is one of the stupidest things you can do as a human being. The facts speak for themselves— over twenty thousand people are killed in the United States every year in alcohol-related car accidents. One in three of these people is a nondrinking victim. Damages from drunk driving accidents and associated legal, clinical, and other expenses amount to about $16 billion a year. And, if this present trend continues, there is a 40 percent chance that you will be involved in an alcohol-related crash at some time in your life.

You don't need to be very drunk to cause an accident. At .05 percent BAC—only one or two drinks for some people—drivers lose inhibitions and feel more relaxed about everything. Someone at this level of intoxication might misjudge the severity of a driving situation and fail to recognize a potential accident until it's too late.

As the BAC increases, driver reflexes deteriorate. At .10 percent BAC, motor areas in the brain become depressed, resulting in slowed reaction times and uncoordinated movements. At this stage, drivers' reflexes may be too slow to respond to a hazardous situation even if they can recognize it.

At higher levels, coordination and judgment deteriorate even further. Drunk drivers also develop vision problems as alcohol affects the delicate muscle structure of the eye. With such poor powers of judgment, motor control, and eyesight, driving at this point is an invitation to tragedy.

The chart on page 187 shows the statistical relationship between BAC levels and automobile accidents:*

Do you remember all those drunk variables—mood, metabolism, age, and so on—listed earlier in the chapter? Taking those into consideration, the figures in this chart reflect the lowest probability for an individual. If a driver feels tired, is

---

*The BAC information here and in the remainder of this section is courtesy of the Mothers Against Drunk Driving.

on medication, has a slow metabolism, a weak liver, or maybe just had a rough day, the chances of accident could skyrocket.

BAC (%)	*Risk of Accident*
.05	2–3 times the normal risk
.08	5–6 times the normal risk
.10	7–8 times the normal risk
above .10	20–50 times the normal risk

What if you do drive and happen to get caught? The consequences depend on where you are at the time. In most states, holding a driver's license means that the authorities have your "implied consent" to give you a Breathalyzer test and to require that you take it. If you refuse, you face prosecution.

The Breathalyzer measures your BAC level. In many states, a .10 percent BAC constitutes per-se evidence of driving under the influence of alcohol—that is, conclusive evidence you were driving drunk. States with a per-se intoxication level of .10 percent include: Alabama, Alaska, Arizona, Arkansas, Colorado, Connecticut, Delaware, District of Columbia, Georgia, Hawaii, Idaho, Illinois, Indiana, Iowa, Kentucky, Louisiana, Michigan, Minnesota, Mississippi, Missouri, Montana, Nebraska, Nevada, New Jersey, New York, North Dakota, Ohio, Oklahoma, Pennsylvania, Rhode Island, South Dakota, Texas, Washington, West Virginia, Wisconsin, and Wyoming.

Eleven states have introduced legislation where the level has been dropped to .08 percent. These states include: California, Florida, Kansas, Maine, New Hampshire, New Mexico, North Carolina, Oregon, Utah, Vermont, and Virginia.

Laws in Maryland, Massachusetts, South Carolina, and Tennessee aren't per-se laws. A BAC of .10 percent (.08 in Massachusetts) is evidence of alcohol impairment but isn't illegal per se.

In addition to these laws, thirty-one states have laws on the books with different DWI levels for underage drinkers.

Underage BAC laws apply to all drinkers younger than twenty-one except in Georgia, Louisiana, North Carolina, Oklahoma, and Vermont where they apply to drivers younger than eighteen. The Wisconsin law applies to drivers younger than nineteen.

State	BAC Level	State	BAC Level
Alaska	.00	New Jersey	.01
Arizona	.00	New Mexico	.02
Arkansas	.02	North Carolina	.00
California	.05	Ohio	.02
District of Columbia	.00	Oklahoma	.02
Georgia	.04	Oregon	.00
Idaho	.02	Rhode Island	.04
Illinois	.00	Tennessee	.02
Louisiana	.04	Texas	.07
Maine	.02	Utah	.00
Maryland	.02	Vermont	.02
Massachusetts	.02	Virginia	.02
Michigan	.02	Washington	.02
Minnesota	.00	West Virginia	.02
Nebraska	.02	Wisconsin	.00
New Hampshire	.04		

If you're stupid enough to drink and drive, find your state in the above lists and follow those legal guidelines. Don't trust these lists for too long, though—the laws are constantly changing, usually in the direction of stricter legislation against drunk driving. Anyway, unless you go to a bar with a Breathalyzer, there's no sure way to measure your BAC. The safest way to protect yourself is to abstain from drinking before driving.

The Bartender's Responsibilities

Why does a bartender need to know so much information about drinking and driving? Remember, judgment is the first response to go in a drinker's brain. How can a person with poor judgment possibly know when to stop drinking if the bartender doesn't step in? Therefore, the bartender should try to keep drinkers sober.

Perhaps concern for your customer's safety and welfare isn't enough to make you go through the hassle of "shutting off" a drunk. It's a lot easier to go on serving intoxicated people to keep them quiet. Besides, drunks often tip better.

Would you feel at least a little bit sorry if your laziness caused a drunken customer to die in an accident or cause other damages? If you answered no to this question, the government and judicial system would like to change your mind. Nationwide, there has been a recent crackdown on drunk driving. On one hand, the crackdown centers on catching and punishing people who drive under the influence of alcohol. Many states have passed stricter laws to deal with these people, including mandatory jail terms in some instances. On the other hand, legislators have recently been coming to the realization that maybe they should go closer to the root of the problem: if people don't get drunk, they won't drive drunk. After a certain point of lost judgment, however, a drinker cannot decide when to stop. Lawmakers would like to help these people by shifting the responsibility of judgment over to the people who serve liquor.

Dram shop legislation stems from this line of thought. Dram shop laws, statutes on the books of many states, make specific provisions to prosecute the servers of drunks. If a person becomes intoxicated and causes damages, either the drunk or someone adversely affected by the drunk's actions can sue the establishment that served the liquor. It is not reserved solely for bars, either. Hosts of private parties have been held liable for damage caused by intoxicated guests.

Many states without dram shop statutes have prosecuted servers of drunks through case law. Suits against bar owners and party hosts established precedents of prosecution for similar subsequent cases.

These laws are getting tougher. In many states, the operator's license may be automatically revoked. In the near future, however, don't be surprised if bartenders must defend themselves legally for damages caused or incurred by their patrons. Be prepared.

How can you protect yourself, your patron, and the bar where you work? For starters, read this chapter carefully to learn how to recognize an intoxicated person. Some bars provide those weight tables to help you decide how much to serve a person, but these aren't very accurate, so be careful. (And remember your bar or your party may be a guest's third stop that day.) Recently, some bars have purchased a Breathalyzer to help patrons decide when to stop drinking and/or call a cab. Since their use remains voluntary, this method has not been too successful, but it's a step in the right direction.

If a person shows signs of intoxication, do not serve that person. Then again, some drinkers can go all night without so much as a slur . . . but then they may get behind the wheel and lose control. To prevent such problems, try to keep track of your customers and don't serve anyone too much, regardless of outward appearance. Unfortunately, this is easier said than done, as many drinkers become belligerent in the face of such humiliation. To avoid unpleasant situations, be very discreet; quietly refuse to serve alcohol, then offer the guest some soda or coffee. With a nonalcoholic drink, the patron probably won't feel so embarrassed at being shut off. If the customer appears dangerously drunk, quietly offer to call a cab. Some people will appreciate your kindness and sensitivity. Some will call you names you never heard of before. If a patron sets off fireworks at the suggestion of a shut-off, you may have to become more forceful; summon the manager to help you, and, if necessary, the police as well. Despite the hassle it might cause you at the time, your responsible, alert attitude toward intoxicated people will probably spare everybody much greater problems later.

If you're the creative type, you might scoff at such boring suggestions. Use your imagination (careful, though!) in throwing out drunks—don't always rely on a discreet soda water or a biceps-bound bouncer to help you out of these situations. John, a graduate of the Harvard Bartending Course, keeps control of every problem with his special weapon: his sense of humor. He works in a busy, crowded bar situated in the center of town, so he can't easily keep count of how many drinks each patron has had, either in his bar or at nearby bars earlier that day. One night, a particularly sloshed patron dropped by after having spent the afternoon at the pub next door. This customer stumbled up to the bar and tried desperately to focus his eyes and unglue his tongue from the top of his mouth to order a drink. As the drunk attempted to steady himself on the edge of a stool, John quipped, "Buddy, I hope you're driving home—you'll never make it walking." The customer got quite a chuckle out of that one, and agreed with John's decision to shut him off. (John thinks "agreed" might be the wrong word. He feels perhaps the customer really had no idea what was going on around him.)

Amanda, another Harvard Bartending grad, agrees with John's philosophy. "Many people who have drunk too much feel pretty jolly, and will respond more readily to a friendly, lighthearted bartender. Nobody likes to be sternly reprimanded or treated like a child." With that in mind, Amanda takes a rather cheerful approach to refusing service. If a customer orders a "Schotch and shoda," she smiles and promises, "When you learn how to say it, the drink's on the house," as she plunks down a glass of water on the bar and walks away. Later she'll come back and quietly offer to call a cab, but she tries to make light of the whole matter to help the customer feel more comfortable. Many patrons even return the next night, order the drink again (this time "Scotch and soda"), and receive their free reward. Sure, a remark like that might get you in trouble with the wrong customer, but Amanda rarely has any problems.

Of the Harvard Bartending grads we talked to, Kate follows the strictest guidelines. "If one of my customers tried to drive home drunk, and ended up killing someone, I couldn't live with myself. I'd feel like a murderer." Motivated by this fear, Kate absolutely refuses to serve liquor to a drunk, and she does it in a very straightforward manner. She immediately calls a bouncer over who then hustles the drinker out of the bar and into a cab. She's seen several customers put up a struggle and has been called many nasty names, but not one of Kate's patrons has ever had an accident.

Minors pose another problem. You probably know the legal drinking age in your state, so do not serve alcohol to minors. Ask for positive identification from all suspected underagers and refuse service if they cannot produce it. If caught serving underage people, a bar might automatically have its license suspended or revoked and be forced to pay hefty fines.

Mark has tended bar for four years since receiving his Harvard Master of Mixology degree. "I don't take any chances. If I find any reason to suspect someone is underage, I throw the kid out. Sometimes I even get the manager just to scare them a little." Mark claims he knows every trick now—sisters' and brothers' IDs, duplicate licenses with the right picture but the wrong name, excuses like "But I left my ID in my other wallet," fake mail-order IDs, school IDs with no date ("That code number there under my picture means I'm twenty-one"), and countless other ploys. Mark also tries to keep an eye out for minors who convince older people to buy drinks for them. "I like my job. This is a great bar. I'm not about to ruin everything just for some punk who wants a drink."

John, Amanda, Kate, and Mark exemplify the Harvard Bartender: they're responsible, alert, and know that bartending doesn't begin and end with just mixing drinks. They are aware of the side effects alcohol may elicit in drinkers and consider such knowledge part of the job. As Mark says, "A pharmacist wouldn't dispense drugs he didn't understand the effects of—neither will I."

CHAPTER 7

Professional Bartending

This IS it—you've patiently learned every trick of the trade. You can set up a bar, throw a good cocktail party, mix any one of a hundred drinks in the blink of an eye, and even converse intelligently about the genealogy of gin. And now, you want what every good American wants—a paycheck.

And why not? Whether you're looking for part-time work or a full-fledged career, bartending can be both a fun and an interesting job. Furthermore, you can make a pretty good living at it in some of the choicer bars. In the first half of this chapter, we'll tell you how to find a job—where and how to look for a place that fits your talents. In the second half, we'll tell you how to act on the job—what to wear, what to do, and what not to do as a professional bartender.

Looking for a Job

High employee turnover makes bartending an ideal job to break into. If you hit the right place at the right time, presto—

Well, okay—it's not quite that easy. Remember how we explained each drink-mixing process as though a two-year-old child could do it? When you start dealing with professionals in real bars, it's not quite that simple. Working in a high-class bar requires speed and efficiency, and the only way you can develop these skills is through experience. No matter how many times you carefully read Chapter 2 or how many drink recipes you diligently memorized in Chapter 3, you will not be able to stroll into the Ritz tomorrow and land a job. Chances are, you'll have to start near the bottom and work your way up.

The good news here is that the bottom of the bartending world isn't necessarily the worst place in the world. You don't have to start out in a miserable spot where the boss is an ape and the customers are baboons. Rather, "bottom" generally refers to places where you won't make much money: the low salaries, poor customers, and empty barrooms won't pay your rent. Compensation for hard work at the bottom comes in the form of the speed, efficiency, and experience you will gain so you can move up to the next, higher-paying tier.

There are a number of different types of businesses that hire bartenders. They are listed below in roughly ascending order according to the amount of experience you need to get hired by them. Keep in mind, however, that this will vary considerably according to the individual business. Extremely posh catering services, for example, will probably be more selective than those that cater to Little League banquets. Of course, most Little League banquets won't require a bartender anyway. . . .

1. Catering or temporary services: Bartending at catered events is usually an undemanding experience, and most caterers are willing to hire people with little or no experience. Unfortunately, tips are not very large at catered events, and you will probably not make a lot of money at these jobs. The best way to find a caterer in your area is to check the Yellow Pages.

2. Hotels with banquet facilities: These are very similar to catering jobs; most are low pressure and low paying. Frequently, hotels will have an office for hiring staff of all varieties and this is the place to inquire about the availability of jobs.

3. Harbor cruises: This option is obviously limited to people who live near large bodies of water. Also known as "booze cruises," these jobs are usually a little more demanding than catering work. Most of the companies that offer these cruises have offices directly on the docks. Tips will vary widely depending on who's renting the boat.

4. Airport/Train station bars: These are also low-pressure jobs. Unfortunately, tipping is usually terrible. Many times these bars are owned by outside corporations that pay rent to the airport/station in exchange for space, so a manager may be harder to track down in person. Be persistent; jobs at these places are easier to come by than you might think.

5. Hotel and restaurant bars: These vary widely depending on the quality of the hotel or restaurant. In larger restaurants, you can find work at the service bar—at these, you'll make drinks to be served by the waiters and waitresses. These provide good experience, but since you won't be in contact with customers, you probably won't get any tips.

6. Local bars without large crowds: These are your typical neighborhood bars—cozy, friendly, and usually very quiet. If there's a strong contingent of "regulars" you may make good tips. However, the less crowded the bar, the fewer tips you'll get.

7. Public bars: These are the large-capacity, crowded bars and nightclubs where customers stand two or three deep at the bar on the weekends and the bartenders are usually run ragged until closing time. These are the highest-paying bartending jobs, but they're also the most demanding. Don't expect to land one of these jobs without experience.

"So how do I get a job at one of these places?" you're probably asking yourself. There is no single method that's guaranteed to be successful; however, there are a few different approaches you can take.

Apply directly to the manager: Find a place that looks appealing, stroll right in, and ask to see the manager. If they're not currently hiring, they might be soon; leave a résumé or make sure the manager knows how to get in touch with you if an opening pops up. Never look for work during peak hours, since both the manager and the rest of the employees will probably be busy preparing and will resent you for interrupting them. The best time to approach a bar looking for work is between three and five in the afternoon, when the manager should be around but won't be too busy. Never ask another bartender if that particular place is hiring; they will almost always say no, regardless of the truth of the matter. This is because the bartender probably has a friend that he or she would like to see hired instead of you if the bar does happen to be hiring.

Use personal connections: As in any job hunt, this should not be underestimated. If you happen to be the friend of the bartender in the above example, you've got a leg up on everyone else who is applying—knowing a current employee who's willing to give you a good recommendation is a definite advantage.

Be willing to start in a position other than bartending: There are essentially two bar jobs other than bartending—working the door and working as a barback. If you're hired by a bar and you don't have much experience, chances are you'll be asked to start at one of these jobs and work your way up to tending bar in a couple of months. Beware of bait-and-switch tactics on the part of the manager. If it becomes apparent that he or she has no intention of promoting you, it might be a good idea to start looking for another job.

Working the door is essentially a dead-end job. You'll be able to pick up a fair amount of knowledge about how a bar is run, but you won't get any hands-on experience. Working as a barback, on the other hand, is a much better way to learn the bartending trade. A barback—also known as a "bar rat" in seedier locales—is essentially an apprentice bartender; your responsibilities will include tapping kegs, running ice, replacing glassware, stocking garnishes, and so on. You'll have the opportunity to observe closely the bartenders that you're backing up—keep your eyes open, file away any questions that come to mind, and ask them whenever there's a lull. If you develop a good relationship with your bartender, you may be asked to set up drinks—that is, put everything in a particular drink except the alcohol. After a few weeks of this type of experience, you should be ready to make the move to bartending.

Offer to take a slow shift: You may not have a choice in this matter. Slow shifts such as lunch bar shifts, Sunday brunches, and possibly Monday or Tuesday nights offer the same pluses and minuses as working in an uncrowded bar; you'll be under less pressure to perform, but your tips won't be big, either.

Don't lie about your experience: Outright lying—or just exaggerating—about your experience may get you a job, but it's not a good idea. Bartending is a learned craft, and if you lie your way into a job that's beyond your experience level, you'll be found out after an hour and quite possibly thrown out on your ear. Furthermore, lying is morally wrong.

Look for seasonal work: Summer and winter tourist spots usually hire many more employees during the high season. The advantages are obvious—not only are there more job opportunities, but you'll probably be working somewhere near either a beach or a ski slope. If you want to find this sort of summer work, start looking far in advance; if, for example, you want a summer job on Cape Cod, start your search when there's still snow on the ground and all the other would-be bartenders are still skiing.

Cruise ships also offer interesting bartending opportunities as long as you're prepared for a major lifestyle change. Most hire out of Miami and New York.

Find out if a local union has a referral service: In some cities, the local Hotel and Restaurant, Institutional Employees and Bartenders Union offers a job referral service to its members. Large hotels, restaurant chains, and other unionized establishments sometimes hire directly through the union, so membership will spare you the tedious door-knocking you'll have to do otherwise. Call your local to inquire; if it doesn't have a referral service, don't bother to join—there's no point in paying union dues when you're unemployed.

Cultivate current employers as references: Never consciously alienate an employer, regardless of what an ogre he or she is. When you're looking for that prestigious second (or third or fourth) job, your potential future employer will want to know how well you performed in your last position. Be prepared to provide names and phone numbers of former employers as references. If you really *did* annoy your last boss, it's probably not a good idea to use him or her as a reference.

Don't get discouraged: Finding a first job can be tedious and frustrating. Above all, don't get discouraged. Be persistent. Speak as politely to the fortieth manager as you did to the first. Emphasize how hard you'll work and how willing you are to accept low pay to gain experience.

Acting Like a Professional

Appearance

Bartending is a service profession, which means that only half the job involves making drinks efficiently. The other half requires that you make people happy—a bartender has to learn how to please both the customer and the managers at the same time.

A clean, spiffy appearance is crucial for professional bartending. In a restaurant, the manager can hide a grubby, slovenly vermin-infested cook back in the kitchen if he has to. By contrast, bartenders work right up front, handling ice and fruit in full view of the customers. Obviously, a good bartender must look immaculate and well groomed; drinks prepared by a sloppy bartender with dirty hands are unappealing.

Most bar managers will tell you what to wear when they hire you; most will request that you wear clothes appropriate for the bar's style. Whatever you wear, always look neat and comfortable so you can maintain a cool, confident bartender image, even after several hectic hours. If you're allowed to choose your dress in a somewhat fancy place or a catering agency, or if you're self-employed, stick with traditional bar attire. Men wear dark pants and shoes with a white shirt and a bow tie. The bow tie idea might sound silly, but long ties have an irritating tendency to fall into the drinks you mix. A bow tie may make you look like Pee Wee Herman but will provide essential freedom of movement. Women should wear a dark skirt or slacks with a white blouse. Long-haired representatives of both sexes should tie their tresses back neatly.

Try to keep your appearance behind the bar as close to neutral as possible. A good bartender is like a good vodka—he or she promotes a pleasant feeling of well-being, but blends easily into many surroundings. Both men and women should avoid wearing flashy jewelry, political buttons, and outrageous clothing—if you have any doubts as to the neutrality of a hair style or article of clothing, do not wear it. Some bars may promote an alternative appearance, but most prefer the more conservative look. Use your own judgment in these matters, but remember—although customers probably won't speak up and tell you when your appearance has offended them, their tips will.

Attitude and Behavior

In a way, this aspect of bartending is more important than anything else. Mix a screwdriver with the wrong amount of vodka, and nobody'll notice. Annoy a customer, and the whole bar hears about it.

Whatever happens, look like you know what you're doing. Nine times out of ten, a confident attitude will fool the customer, even if you have no idea what goes in a rum and Coke. If you maintain that image of authority, patrons won't question your ability to mix a drink or your decision to shut off a drunk. Customers and bar managers get uncomfortable when they see their bartender stumbling around looking noticeably confused, or scowling and muttering irritably. Always smile (or at least look cocky), grab bottles by the neck surely and swiftly, speak clearly and positively, and act like you know every drink ever invented.

That last word of wisdom needs a bit of clarification. Don't feel mortified if you must ask the customer what goes in a drink. You should feel properly stupid if you don't know how to make a gin and tonic, but nobody expects you to remember what goes into a Pink Squirrel. Don't be afraid to ask, and don't rule out the possibility of bluffing a bit since the customer probably doesn't even know the ingredients of the really exotic drinks. Why embarrass him or her by asking?

If you do completely screw up a drink, you can usually talk your way out of it. One former instructor of the Harvard Bartending Course used to tell the following tale: once, when he was just beginning his illustrious career, a customer ordered a Hop-Skip-and-Go-Naked. The instructor vaguely remembered that the drink must be pretty strong to merit such a name, so he confidently sauntered to the back bar, threw in a little of this, a dash of that, a few ounces of flavored brandies, some coloring, several rums, and three garnishes. He presented the masterpiece with a flourish to the customer, who stared at the concoction in horror and protested, "But that's not one-ounce vodka, one-ounce gin, and the juice from half a lime, filled with beer!" Without missing a beat, the instructor replied, "Oh, you wanted a *Western* Hop-Skip-and-Go-Naked. I made you the Eastern version!"

Don't forget that line—you may need it some day. Many drinks change drastically from one region of the country to another or even from one bar to another. Just try to keep on top of the variations as much as possible and act confident even when you're not.

The Customer Is Always Right, Even When Stupid

However painful it may be to follow this axiom in practice, the customer is always right. If a patron accuses you of making a drink improperly, at least go through the motions of altering it according to his or her wishes. Sometimes a difficult customer has had a hard day or just wants a little more attention, or happens to be a complete jerk. Never say, "No, you're wrong. The recipe for a White Russian does not call for mayonnaise." Nobody ever got rich by taking the moral high ground.

Always treat customers courteously; never hurry them or show irritation. The moment a customer arrives, you should spring into action: smile, greet the guest warmly, and drop whatever you were doing to wait on him or her. Try to remember the faces (names, if introduced) and tastes of your regular customers so you can ask if they went "the usual" as soon as they come in. This is very clichéd but is also very much appreciated by most customers.

Be aware of whom you talk to and when. Never appear to be listening in on a conversation or trying to take part. As soon as you have served a drink, step back from the customer or move away. Some folks will want to talk to you . . . desperately. You'll quickly learn to spot those people, and if you bartend long enough, you'll probably devise ingenious ways of avoiding long conversations about their personal problems. On the other hand, a couple having a personal argument doesn't want to hear your opinion on the matter, so give them a wide berth. If invited to chat with someone for a moment, never talk about another customer or gossip about scandals you've witnessed at the bar—including your own; it's safer and more professional to leave your personal life at home.

If you must answer a telephone at the bar, do so quietly. If the call is for a patron, never say the person is there. Instead, offer to inquire, and leave it up to the customer to decide whether to answer the phone.

Customers who smoke should be indulged regardless of the medical consequences. If a customer reaches for a cigarette, light it. Replace ashtrays regularly and correctly: put a clean ashtray over the dirty one and lift both from the bar (to avoid scattering ashes all over the place), then place the clean tray on the bar.

Ultimately, you should do everything in your power to make sure your customers are happy. Learn which customers—both as individuals and, if you work in a bar without established regulars, as stereotypes—like to be pampered and which like to be left more or less alone when their glass is not empty. The bottom line is tips: your aim is to maximize the tips you make, and the happier the customer is, the larger the tip.

Yes, Boss. Right Away, Ma'am. Anything You Say, Sir.

Bartenders who offend customers just lose their tips. Bartenders who offend the boss lose their jobs. Of course, one way to offend the boss is to offend the customers—but if the customer is always right, the boss is always just a little bit more right. Managers expect all bartenders, even beginners, to adhere to a set of commonsense guidelines. Therefore, if you want to keep your job, get raises, work better shifts, and earn a flattering job reference, you'd best impress the boss.

Managers and customers think highly of a busy, hardworking bartender. Even during a lull period, you can always find plenty to do around the bar: wipe spills, wash glasses, clean ashtrays, cut fruit, make premixes (such as sour mix and Bloody Mary mix) and pick up dirty glasses, straws, and napkins. Even when you talk to customers, look busy and you'll make a good impression on everybody.

Even if you don't hit that lull period, take a few seconds here and there to keep the bar clean. Customers won't want to drink at a messy, littered bar, so managers always frown upon a slob behind the bar.

If you're looking for the quickest, easiest way to get fired, try cheating on your boss. Bar managers have usually worked in the business for a long time and can tell when a bartender takes a few dollars here and there or serves free drinks to friends. In fact, managers even notice when a bartender has a heavy hand with liquor bottles. If inventories fall especially low after a certain bartender's shift, that person has poured too much into each drink. Be stingy. Also be thrifty regarding which brands you use. In most operations, you'll be told to put the cheapest ("house" or "bar") brand in a drink unless the customer requests a "call" (name) brand.

If you want to get canned *really* fast, have a few drinks. Drinking on the job makes you an inefficient bartender and proves you have no respect for the boss or the customers. All you have to do is spill a drink, slur a few words, and insult a customer—before you can even hiccup, you'll get fired faster than Billy Martin used to.

As you shower your boss with attention, don't ignore co-workers. Treat them with courtesy, too. Make sure to leave the bar clean, orderly, and well stocked with supplies at the end of your shift. If someone asks you to fill in for a shift, do so whenever possible. Of course, co-workers can't fire you for an unpleasant disposition, but bar work is much more fun when employees get along well and help each other.

Passing the Bucks

Proficiency in money handling requires practice. In a busy bar, many errors result from giving change for the wrong amount of money, such as when a bartender mistakes a ten-dollar bill for a twenty. To minimize these errors, follow the process of the "5 Cs": collect cash; call it; cash register; correct till-slot; count change back.

1. *Collect cash:* So you don't forget in the confusion of a busy bar, collect the money for a drink right after you serve it. (If your bar has a tab or check system the manager will teach you the correct procedure to follow.)

2. *Call it:* "Call" the amount of money. When the customer hands you the bill, say "That's two-fifty out of ten." You'll be more likely to remember exactly what you have.

3. *Cash register:* Keep the bill on top of the cash register until you hand the customer the change. You will remember what amount to make change from, and will be protected if the customer insists, "But I gave you a twenty-dollar bill, not a ten."

4. *Correct till-slot:* Get in the habit of putting each denomination in the correct till-slot of the cash register. Then, if the customer says you counted the change wrong, check the register to see if you put the bill in the wrong slot.

5. *Count change back:* Count the change back to the customer, saying "Two-fifty out of ten: here's fifty cents for three dollars, two more to make five, and five more makes ten," as you hand back the money.

If you cannot satisfactorily handle a customer complaint, call the manager. Usually, money complications become the manager's responsibility. Don't be insulted, however, if the manager returns the customer's money without question— remember, the customer is always right. If a similar problem occurs involving the same customer a second time, you and the manager should proceed cautiously. You're probably getting suckered.

You will also have to handle tip money in a bar. Some places pool all the tips earned in a given shift and then split the money equally among all the bartenders. This method is equitable when bartenders share areas and, therefore, customers.

Never announce the amount of a tip, no matter how great or small. It's embarrassing to the customer. Not only that, it's very tacky.

But Ossifer, I Feel Wonnerful. . .

Protect yourself and your employer. Read the section in Chapter 6 on the bartender's responsibility carefully. Given changing judicial attitudes toward liability, bartenders and managers are forced these days to assume more responsibility for the people they serve. If you do your job right, you will probably have to cut off a drunk from time to time. This is not much fun, but it is considerably more fun than losing a liquor license, paying a massive fine, or doing time.

Well, that's all, folks, You now know all you'll ever need to become one of the nation's bartending elite. So get out there and start mixing those drinks! Before you do, however, test your knowledge against our grueling Bar Exam. . .

The Bar Exam

So, do you feel pretty knowledgeable now? Are you mixing Manhattans with your eyes closed and throwing fêtes for your friends at the drop of a hat? Or did you just skip to the back of the book to see how it ends? Either way, you should take a crack at our Bar Exam. Developed by the same team of mean-spirited, cranky old men who designed those multiple-choice science tests in high school, it's guaranteed to challenge the outer limits of your bartending skills.

1. The first ingredient that always goes into a highball is:
    a. milk
    b. ice
    c. love

2. An extra-dry martini:
    a. contains very little vermouth
    b. does not sweat, even when nervous
    c. is like a dry martini, only with a better marketing plan

3. A fifth is:
    a. the last set of a close one at Wimbledon
    b. twenty percent
    c. ⅕ gallon or ⅘ quart

4. A Manhattan is:
    a. a drink with burgeoning social problems
    b. four parts blended whiskey, one part sweet vermouth
    c. a better movie than *Annie Hall*

5. A Godfather is:
    a. usually a close friend of the parents
    b. 1½ oz. bourbon or blended whiskey, ½ oz. amaretto
    c. well-dressed, Sicilian, and extremely influential

6. A one-man bar is best suited for:
    a. parties of 15 to 100 people
    b. misanthropes
    c. monogamous drinkers

7. If you will be bartending at a party for senior citizens, and the hostess asks you for advice in liquor selection, you should suggest:
    a. something that mixes well with prune juice
    b. running with a younger crowd
    c. ordering more dark alcohol

8. A Cape Codder is:
    a. vodka and cranberry juice
    b. a vacationing WASP
    c. cold and aloof, unless he's introduced by the right person

9. A garnish is:
   a. an adjective used to describe garns
   b. sort of like paint
   c. a section of fruit or vegetable added to a drink

10. A dry Manhattan is:
    a. New York City, 1920–1933
    b. A party at Bill Buckley's town house
    c. A regular Manhattan, but with dry vermouth instead of sweet

Exam Answer Key

1. b
2. a
3. c
4. b
5. b
6. a
7. c
8. a
9. c
10. c

Give yourself one point for each right answer. Subtract 40 points for each wrong answer. If you scored a positive number, you passed! If you scored a negative number, you should try again—only this time, do yourself a favor. Cheat.

Graduation

Did you pass the bar exam? Of course you did! Now get out there and start mixing those drinks! You crazy kids! Use the form at the back of this book to order your very own bartending kit.

INDEX

Page references in italics denote diagrams and illustrations.

A. BARTENDING KIT

Comes with everything you need to be a successful bartender! Shaker, mixing glass, strainer, bar spoon, jigger/pony, corkscrew, and six speedpourers. $29.95

B. EXTRA SPEEDPOURERS

For your expanding bar needs. Package of six. $3.25

Prices subject to change.

- -

ORDER FORM

ITEM	QTY	AMT

A.   BARTENDING KIT: $29.95 plus $5.00 postage and handling.   (Mass. residents add 5% sales tax.) ___ ___

b. EXTRA SPEED-POURERS: $3.25 (Mass. residents add 5% sales tax.) ___ ___

TOTAL: _____

Name _____
Address
(no. & street) _____

City/State/Zip _____

Telephone (   ) _____

Enclose a check or
money order payable to:

Harvard Bartending Course
HARVARD STUDENT AGENCIES, INC.
53-A Church St.
Cambridge, Ma. 02138
(617) 495–3033